# RICH GOD POOR GOD

By John Avanzini

Abel Press
Tulsa, Oklahoma

*Rich God Poor God*
ISBN: 1-878605-43-7

Unless otherwise indicated, all Scripture quotations are taken from the *King James Version* of the Bible.

Verses marked Amplified are Scripture taken from THE AMPLIFIED BIBLE, Old Testament copyright © 1965, 1987 by The Zondervan Corporation. The Amplified New Testament copyright © 1958, 1987 by The Lockman Foundation. Used by permission.

Verses marked NIV are taken from the Holy Bible: New International Version © 1978 by the New York International Bible Society, used by permission.

Scripture quotations marked NKJV are taken from *The New King James Version*. Copyright © 1979, 1980, Nelson, Inc.

Scripture quotations marked NLT are taken from the Holy Bible, New Living Translation, copyright © 1996. Used by permission of Tyndale House Publishers, Inc., Wheaton, Illinois 60189. All rights reserved.

Verses marked TLB are taken from *The Living Bible*. Copyright © 1971. Used by permission of Tyndale House Publishers, Inc., Wheaton, Illinois 60189. All rights reserved.

For emphasis, the author has placed selected words from the Bible quotations in italics.

**Abel Press**
**P.O. Box 702357**
**Tulsa, Oklahoma 74170-2357**

# CONTENTS

# DEDICATION

Dedicated to Cesar and Sherry Brooks, pastors of First Family Church of Augusta, Georgia, who encouraged me to write this book.

# INTRODUCTION

Imagine a wealthy father whose abundant riches are so great that no one can even begin to guess his net worth. Everyone believes this father to be kind, generous and loving. In fact, even perfect strangers testify to this father's desire to provide the good life for those who serve him.

However, a paradox exists, for many of the children of this most wealthy father sincerely believe he expects them to live meagerly instead of abundantly. They feel they must dwell in mortgaged homes with debt weighing heavily upon their shoulders, hopelessly enslaved to lack and continual need. While faithfully praising the goodness of their father, they never seem to break out of the paralyzing grip of insufficiency. All of this takes place while their rich father's wealth continues to compound, and they fall further and further behind, accumulating bill upon bill, credit card upon credit card, and debt upon debt.

To make matters worse, whenever a special opportunity for the advancement of the father's aggressive expansion program arises, his children must all generously chip in to pay for the new program. They continually encourage one another to scrimp and scrape to fund these special advancement projects for their rich father. These children sincerely believe that it's up to them to provide for their father's dream of world evangelism.

Would you call this father loving, kind or generous? I think not. In fact, when a father in today's culture fails to provide for his children, he is called *abusive* and *uncaring*. The courts often force such rogue fathers to pay child support, attaching their wages to assure that their children's needs are properly met. In plain words, the court of public opinion would brand this father's actions as blatant *child abuse*.

How strange it must seem to the lost people of this world that the notoriously rich God of heaven would so poorly provide for His own children!

Now here is the truth of the matter:

As children of God, we have a heavenly Father who "owns the cattle on a thousand hills" (Psalm 50:10). The rich God of the Scripture openly declares, *"The silver is mine, and the gold is mine, saith the LORD of hosts"* (Haggai 2:8). Everyone knows the real God has limitless assets. However, much too often His children declare to the world by their diminished lifestyles that He should be classified as a poor god! They are constantly using every possible means to raise funds for their various projects, while they go without the things they need in their personal lives. The thinking folks of this world ask, and rightly so, "How is it possible that a truly rich Father would have so many poor children?"

I ask you again, how can this be when Abraham, the earthly father of the Judeo-Christian faith, calls the God of heaven *Jehovah Jireh,* the one who abundantly provides for His children (Genesis 22:14)? Contrary to this truth, these poverty-minded saints should rename their god Jehovah Needy, the god whose children provide for him. With this in mind, please allow me to ask you the following questions:

- Are you presenting to the world that your God is rich or poor?

- Is your Heavenly Father Jehovah Jireh (the God who provides) or Jehovah Needy (the god whose children provide for him)?

## — YOU WILL HAVE THE GOD YOU PERCEIVE —

In this book, you will discover that the Bible teaches *you will have the God you perceive,* just like the mistaken steward in the Parable of the Talents (Matthew 25:24-26). This wicked steward believed his god to be harsh, cruel, unfair and stingy. Please notice that without as much as a word of opposition to the steward's wrong conclusion, his master allowed him to continue in his error. This mistaken servant had to live with the self-serving god that his flawed theology had given to him.

The actual truth of this parable is that the master was rich not poor, generous not stingy, fair not unfair. Sadly, the misinformed steward never learned his master's true nature. This mistake caused the steward's *perception* of his master to become his *reality.*

In Matthew 25:24-26 the mistaken servant perceived God as a taker. Carefully listen to his words as he describes his master.

**Thou art a hard man, reaping where thou hast not sown. . . .**

**Matthew 25:24**

This is not an accurate reflection of God's true nature, for God Jehovah never reaps where He doesn't sow. Instead, the exact opposite is true. God is faithful to give generous harvests where His children have sown.

In spite of the tremendous weight of scriptural proof that shows God's unparalleled generosity, many Christians insist on projecting to the world that their God is barely able to provide the resources they need. Listen to the Word of God as it openly declares God's inward desire for the well being and prosperity of His children.

> . . . his divine power hath given unto us *all* things that pertain unto *life* and *Godliness*, through the knowledge of him. . . .
>
> **2 Peter 1:3**

> Let them shout for joy, and be glad, that favour my righteous cause: yea, let them *say continually,* Let the LORD be magnified, which hath *pleasure in the prosperity of his* servant.
>
> **Psalm 35:27**

Through His goodness to His children, the rich God of heaven reveals to the lost world that He loves them and wants to bring them into the good life.

### Which God Do You Serve?

Take a brief moment to give yourself this test. Answer yes or no to each question.

### What Do You Believe?

Do you believe:

_____ 1. While the streets of heaven are paved with gold, your Heavenly Father would not want you to have much gold or silver while here on earth?

_____ 2. While the house of God is decked out in splendor, your home should be only a humble hut?

_____ 3. Life is simply a journey to get to heaven, and none of heaven's beauty and riches are available to you along the way?

_____ 4. While you are on the journey to heaven, you must sacrifice the truly good things of this life every step of the way?

_____ 5. You must watch your pennies, constantly limiting yourself so that you will have enough excess money to do your part in supporting God's plan for world evangelism?

_____ 6. Each time you hear an evangelistic appeal, you want to give, but you just never seem to have enough money to do it the way you really desire?

If you answered yes to most of these questions, you are projecting to the world that your god is poor!

— BECOMING THE CHILD OF THE RICH GOD —

If you would like to start projecting to this lost and dying world that your God is a good God—one who loves them and is willing to generously provide for them—just keep on reading. This book will show you how to:

- **Be set free** from the bondage of traditional religion's poor-god syndrome.

- **Be delivered** from the ongoing burden of having to continually bail out a needy god.

- **Be enlightened** to God's plan for you to have abundant blessings in this life as well as in the next life.

- **Be released** from the deceptions of organized religion.

- **Become re-acclimated** to living in the abundant environment of Eden, which has been God's desire for you since the beginning of time.

- **Be truly transformed** by the rich God's Son to experience new life in Christ, a more abundant life.

- **Learn how** to take dominion over this world's corrupt religious system instead of serving it as a slave.

- **Be prepared** to witness a harvest-proportion increase on the monies you sow into the good ground of true world evangelism.

- **Be abundantly blessed** by your Heavenly Father who promises to provide you with exceedingly abundantly more than you can ask or think.

Child of God, *this is your moment* in God's plan to leave behind the past lies of the enemy and lay hold on the abundant inheritance that God has prepared for you!

I invite you to join me in seeing God's Word with new eyes. I want to show you that God has promised a generous portion of this world's great wealth to you and your loved ones.

> **Behold, what I have seen to be good and fitting is for one to**
> **eat and drink, and to find enjoyment in all the labor in which he**

labors under the sun all the days which God gives him—for this is his [*alloted*] *part.*

Also, every man to whom God has given riches and possessions, and the power to enjoy them and to accept his appointed lot and to rejoice in his toil—*this is the gift of God* [to him].

**Ecclesiastes 5:18,19 Amplified**

*The good life is a gift from our generous Father.*
*It is both abundant life now and eternal life throughout the endless ages.*

# SLAVES TO A POOR GOD

## CHAPTER 1

Before confessing Jesus Christ as Lord and Savior, we are all slaves to sin. The bondage of sin is brutal, and it is characterized by lives filled with despair, frustration, hopelessness, doubt, and worry. The harsh taskmaster of sin is ever ready to measure out punishment upon the slaves under his control. The wicked master of sinners demands complete obedience and allegiance, promising punishment to any that dare to disobey.

- Drug addicts who try to gain release from their addictions are instantly wracked with withdrawal pains.

- Embezzlers who want to confess and start over cannot because of the paralyzing fear that comes upon them.

- Abusers of other people are continually tortured by their own self-loathing.

- Deceived millions are destined to live under the ongoing pain of inwardly knowing they are being relentlessly stalked by poverty.

We are set free from this evil slave master when the gospel of Jesus Christ sheds light upon our lives. Then, in one marvelous instant, freedom becomes available to the newborn child of God!

We no longer have to be subject to the oppression of the demonic host.

With this wonderful opportunity that Jesus bought and paid for with His precious blood, why is it that so many Christians continue to live in lack and insufficiency? Why don't they come into the full liberty God promises to all that receive Him? Most of these wonderful people are still deceived by some unseen influence that continually tries to take everything they have away from them. These uninformed Christians unwittingly continue to live the lifestyle that their former god had laid out for them. While their eternal destiny has no doubt changed, they still live their present existence in the same insufficiency that dominated them before they met Jesus. They are plagued with despair, hopelessness, poverty and lack, continually suffering defeat and disappointment.

The harsh truth is, these defeated Christians have left one form of slavery only to enter into another. Unwittingly, they have been tricked into perceiving their god as harsh and unfeeling toward them, a god who always demands and seldom gives. They serve their poorly funded churches as slaves, secretly dreading the next expansion program or building push. The unspoken question they are constantly asking themselves is *"How much will this cost?"* These unfortunate saints are often impoverished and steeped in debt, living from week to week on the meager promise of "pie in the sky in the sweet by and by." They go from day to day with no hope for anything much beyond their immediate needs. As they are asked to give again and again, they can't help but wonder where it will come from this time.

## — SERVANTS OR SLAVES? —

The Apostle Paul carefully referred to himself as a "servant of Jesus Christ" (Romans 1:1). We know from his life's work as it is recorded in the New Testament that he was completely sold out to Jesus. Yet Paul referred to himself as a servant, not a slave. A servant functions in voluntary service, unlike a slave who has no choice in the matter. A servant can come and go, whereas a slave must remain.

Do you feel like a slave to your god? Are you always scrimping and scraping to make ends meet? Do you toil long hours to accomplish your god's many requirements for service? Do you find yourself wondering if what you have done is really enough to please the people he has placed over you? If you answered yes to any of these questions, you are about to find freedom that will break the deception that has you shackled to a substandard Christian life. This revelation from God's own Word will release you to live like a real child of the King!

## — YOUR PERCEPTION AND PROJECTION OF GOD —

Perception is not necessarily reality. Just because you perceive something a certain way doesn't mean it is really that way. Consider this example of how misleading your perception can be. If five blindfolded men tried to describe an elephant, they could not do an adequate job, even if each one carefully described the part he was touching. One might describe the tail as a broom, or the leg as a tree. The trunk might feel like a hose and the ear like a fan. Maybe the elephant's side would seem like a large wall. These perceptions would be incorrect in defining a true composite picture of the elephant.

In that same way, if your perception of God comes from *blind guides,* your view of Him will be distorted.

**. . . if the blind lead the blind, both shall fall into the ditch.**

**Matthew 15:14**

It is a fact that those who perceive and project God as poor must live with the consequences that come from serving a poor god. However, those who perceive and project God as rich will live with the abundant provisions of the rich God.

— NEED-BASED GIVING —

It is also a fact that those who perceive God as one that desires them to barely get by will usually give their money only when there is a project that is designated as a *need*. This mentality causes them to give sacrificially to the church building fund so they can help provide the facility they believe their god so desperately needs. However, because of their lack of sufficient surplus funds, after the structure is completed, they will have to turn a deaf ear to the everyday necessities such as tuning the piano or painting the building when needed. They see insufficiency in everything they do. These slaves to the poor god are always trying to find cheaper ways of accomplishing things for their god. Whether or not they realize it, their lifestyles of constant insufficiency loudly proclaim to the world that their god is Jehovah Needy not Jehovah Jireh.

Let it be known to all that the God and Father of our Lord Jesus Christ is rich not poor, sufficient not needy. He gives abundantly to His children and does not grab everything He can from them. Know also that He boldly proclaims His desire for His children to give liberally so that He, the God of abundant provision, may liberally add to their wealth. This enables them to easily fund every joint effort God desires to undertake with them.

**. . . God is able to make all grace abound toward you; that ye, always having all sufficiency in all things, *may abound to every good work.***

**1 Corinthians 9:8**

## — THE RICH GOD GIVES, THE POOR GOD TAKES —

Your perception of God will determine how you relate to Him. To understand this truth more clearly, let's examine the parable of the talents from the Book of Matthew. The steward with one talent perceives (believes in his heart) that his master is a harsh, greedy, and unjust man (Matthew 25:24). However, the Bible plainly states that the master in this parable is a good and generous lord.

**For the kingdom of heaven is as a man traveling into a far country, who called his own servants, and *delivered unto them his goods.***

**And unto one he gave five talents, to another two, and to another one; to every man according to his several ability; and straightway took his journey.**

**Matthew 25:14,15**

Let's begin by allowing our Lord to establish the true nature of this master. Jesus tells us that he is a *giver* not a taker. The Lord plainly states that the master *delivered unto the servants his own goods.* He gave one five talents, another two, and another one. Nowhere does this parable state that the master wanted to take anything away from his servants.

The master in this parable is obviously a type of God the Father, the rich God who generously gives to His children, never desiring to take anything from them.

> **For the kingdom of heaven is as a man traveling into a far country, who called his own servants, and delivered unto them his goods.**
>
> **Matthew 25:14**

He is Jehovah Jireh, the one who promises to provide substance and wealth to His children. Instead of merely giving to God's programs of expansion, the obedient children of God willingly sow their financial seeds into His good-ground ministries. Because of their sowing, they receive financial harvests that give them the funds they need to truly experience the joy of harvest that He promises.

> **Yes, God will give you much so that you can give away much . . . .**
>
> **2 Corinthians 9:11 TLB**

Be honest with yourself. *Do those around you perceive your God to be a giver or a taker?* Is he one who provides or one who impoverishes? One who demands provision *from* you or one who abundantly supplies provision *to* you?

Notice the master in this parable does not say, "Take your hard-earned wages and give them to me." Instead, the master *graciously gives his goods* to his servants, entrusting them with the privilege of handling his money. He trusts them to be his representatives. They know their master's desires and how he wants them to handle the money he has so graciously given them.

Let's examine the difference between the poor god and the rich God and the difference between being a trusted steward or being little more than a slave.

- The poor god continually demands that his slaves give him an ever-increasing part of their meager goods.

- THE RICH GOD ENTRUSTS HIS STEWARDS WITH AN EVER-INCREASING PORTION OF HIS GOODS.

- The poor god distrusts his servants when it comes to money matters. This is obvious from the fact that He severely limits the amount of excess funds he allows them to have.

- THE RICH GOD CONTINUES TO ENTRUST HIS STEWARDS WITH AN EVER-INCREASING AMOUNT OF WEALTH AND INFLUENCE AS THEY PROVE THEMSELVES TRUSTWORTHY IN REDISTRIB-UTING THE THINGS HE PLACES IN THEIR HANDS.

Are you beginning to get the picture? God wants to trust you. He wants to help you manage wealth in such a way that you will be able to bless all the families of the earth!

> **. . . thou shalt be a blessing:**

> **And I will bless them that bless thee, and curse him that curseth thee: and *in thee shall all families of the earth be blessed.***

> **Genesis 12:2,3**

Let the following scriptures establish in you the wonderful truth that the God of heaven is a generous giver.

> **For God so loved the world, that he *gave* his only begotten Son. . . .**

> **John 3:16**

It is an unchanging truth that the supreme, ultimate gift comes from the rich God who unselfishly gave the world His best, His only Son, Jesus Christ!

The rich God of heaven is on the record about His generosity in giving, for He declares that He has set aside a generous portion of this world's wealth for every human being on planet earth.

Behold that which I have seen: it is good and comely for one
to eat and to drink, and to enjoy the good of all his labour that he
taketh under the sun all the days of his life, which God *giveth* him:
for it is his *portion.*

Every man also to whom God hath *given* riches and wealth,
and hath given him power to eat thereof, and to take his *portion,*
and to rejoice in his labour; this is the *gift of God.*

**Ecclesiastes 5:18,19**

Think about it. These verses boldly declare that the rich God
of heaven is a giver not a taker, for He graciously promises every
day of your life to give you:

- All you will ever need to eat and drink

- Full time employment and joy in the fruit of your labor

- More than enough wealth and riches to accomplish His plan
  for your life

- An unending stream of joy in your heart

In others words, one of the rich God's top priorities is to give
you the good life. The Apostle John bears witness to this fact when
he declares that his top prayer for all of God's children is that they
prosper and be in good health.

Beloved, I *wish [pray]* above all things that thou mayest
prosper and be in health, even as thy soul prospereth.

**3 John 2**

Best of all, the Lord Jesus Himself backs this up when He
declares His unselfish purpose for coming to planet earth.

. . . I am come that they might *have life,* and that they might have it *more abundantly.*

**John 10:10**

*The good life is a gift from our generous father. It is both abundant life now and eternal life throughout the endless ages.*

One of the greatest truths about the rich God of heaven is that He doesn't expect His children to supply His needs. Notice this truth in light of Scripture.

**If I [God] were hungry, I would not tell thee, for the world is mine, and the fullness thereof.**

**Psalm 50:12**

The Apostle Paul writes the rest of this story when he tells us whose responsibility it is to do the supplying in the relationship between God the Father and His children.

**But my *God shall supply* all your need according to his riches in glory by Christ Jesus.**

**Philippians 4:19**

Carefully notice that he doesn't say God's children will supply all of the Father's needs according to the abundance of their sweat and toil.

Scripture abounds with verses that loudly proclaim God is a giver. It is His very nature to give. Therefore, if you are properly progressing in the process of being recreated into His image, you will find a new nature growing in you that will turn you into the same kind of giver than your Heavenly Father is. However, if you have somehow been tricked into believing that your god is a taker, subconsciously you will begin to conform to this misconceived image of God. This misconception will cause you to steadily become more and more of a taker.

The children of the rich God know beyond any shadow of doubt that their God is a *giver* and because of this knowledge, they are also becoming *givers*.

## — DOES LOVE OR FEAR MOTIVATE YOU? —

Remember the truth of the parable of the talents; *you will have the god you perceive.* If you perceive God's program to be overrun with need, you will feel the necessity to give only where the need is the greatest.

Not only that, but your perception of God dictates how you manage riches. If you perceive your god to be constantly in need, you will tend to be over cautious, releasing no more of your meager assets than absolutely necessary. The reason is that you will believe the poor god you serve may at any moment fall upon even harder times and look to you to once again bail him out. The perception of those who serve the poor god is that he is primarily a reaper.

You might ask, "Where do you come up with all of this?" It's simple. Jesus tells us about it.

> Then he that had received the five talents went and traded with the same, and made them other five talents.
>
> And likewise he that had received two, he also gained other two.
>
> But he that had received one went and digged in the earth, and hid his lord's money.
>
> **Matthew 25:16-18**

Jesus says the first two servants correctly perceive their master to be a rich and trusting provider. Because of their perception, they prove to be faithful stewards of that which he gives them. They are confident their master is a good, generous, loving lord. They perceive him to be a *giver* not a taker. Out of love, they wisely use that which he entrusts to them to increase the kingdom of their benevolent lord.

However, the misinformed, one-talent servant perceives himself to be the slave of a hard, unjust and self-serving master. Out of fear, this steward hides his lord's money. Understanding his master to be greedy, this slave selfishly holds on to everything he gets his hands on.

The poor slave never learned the divine truth that there can be no harvest unless something is sown. Neither can there be any increase until something is released! Fearfully guarding his meager little handful, the foolish slave hides his money, dreading the wrath of his master whom he perceives to be harsh, unjust, and self-serving.

Consider for a moment the many things you desperately hold on to because of your fear of losing them. Yet Jesus declares that whosoever will gain his life (his soul and the things pertaining to the natural realm) shall lose it, but whosoever will lose his life for Christ's sake will gain life (Matthew 10:39). The amazing truth of all of this is that a real steward has absolutely nothing to lose, for everything God places under your control already belongs to God. Only in giving, releasing, and sowing will you ever be able to fully realize the true purpose for the abundance God has so richly promised to provide.

The misinformed servant never realized that the money his master placed in his hand was not his harvest; it was merely his seed!

**For God . . . will give you more and more seed to plant. . . .**

**2 Corinthians 9:10 TLB**

If you live a life of holding on to everything, be assured that one day you will stand before the Master of your stewardship, totally ashamed of the way you handled God's money.

**It is possible to give away and become richer! It is also possible to hold on too tightly and lose everything. Yes, the liberal man shall be rich! By watering others, he waters himself.**

**Proverbs 11:24,25 TLB**

Wouldn't it be wonderful if the Church would just drop the destructive tradition of poverty and do what Jesus tells us to do? Wealth and prosperity would break forth in the Church like never before. The increase of wealth would be so large that even the heathen would have to declare that the rich God of heaven is at the basis of that which we believe.

**". . . Try it! Let me prove it to you! Your crops will be large, for I will guard them from insects and plagues. Your grapes won't shrivel away before they ripen," says the Lord of Hosts. "And all nations will call you blessed, for you will be a land sparkling with happiness. These are the promises of the Lord of Hosts."**

**Malachi 3:10-12 TLB**

**Give, and it will be given to you. A good measure, pressed down, shaken together and running over, will be poured into your lap. For with the measure you use, it will be measured to you.**

**Luke 6:38 NIV**

That's exactly what happened to the five-talent and two-talent stewards of the parable. With the same measure that they gave, their lord generously multiplied it back to them.

The first two stewards perceived their master to be a rich and generous giver. When he gave his money into their care, they immediately put it to work accomplishing his purposes. Here's the bottom line of their great success. They simply imitated their master's generous nature.

What motivated them to portray to those around them a giving, trustworthy nature? It was the fact that they perceived their lord as generous, caring, and trustworthy. They simply imitated their master.

> ***Therefore be imitators*** **of God [copy Him and follow His example], as well-beloved children [imitate their father].**

> **Ephesians 5:1 Amplified**

All Bible believers know they are made in God's image and possess His basic nature. If you see a Christian acting fearful, he no doubt perceives his God as fearful. However, when the world observes Christians who are generous, liberally giving into every good work, they immediately perceive their God as rich and generous. Their generous lifestyle openly declares to the world that they serve the rich God of the Bible. Read it from God's own Word.

> **Let your light so shine before men, that they may see your good works, and glorify your Father which is in heaven.**

> **Matthew 5:16**

This verse clearly tells us to live our lives before men in such a good and generous way that they will see in us the love of God and His generosity, causing them to glorify God.

You have had the privilege of being in the presence of your Heavenly Father since your new life in Christ began. You have witnessed the extravagance of His creation. You know your Heavenly Father's goodness. If for some reason you have missed the truth that your good God is also a rich God who is pleased to see His children prosper, this error has, no doubt, come about by some mistaken religious tradition.

So please keep on reading and believing, for each sentence of truth from God's Word will draw you closer to the realization that God wants you to prosper. Yes, your God is rich, and your Bible plainly states that it would give Him pleasure to make you rich.

> . . . **Let the LORD be magnified, which hath** *pleasure in the prosperity of his servant.*
>
> *Psalm 35:27*

It is a divine truth that God responds in a positive way to each of His servants who properly use His money. Hear Him as He says, "Well done, good and faithful servant; thou hast been *faithful over a few things,* I will make thee *ruler over many things. . ."* (Matthew 25:21,23).

However, to the fearful servant who mistakenly perceives his master to be hard and selfish, I want you to carefully notice his master does not argue with him. Neither does he try to correct his servant's misconception of him. Instead the master allows him to remain in his deception.

> . . . **thou knowest that I reap where I sowed not, and gather where I have not strawed [scattered seed].**
>
> **Matthew 25:26**

Here we see that God freely allows people to have the god they perceive!

## — I KNEW YOU WERE A HARD MAN —

Notice how stubbornly the one-talent servant hangs on to the misconception of his master's true nature. He continues in error, even though everything the master had ever done for him was kind, loving and generous. In spite of this, he continues to believe just the opposite of the truth.

> **"Then the man with the $1,000 came and said, 'Sir, I knew you were a hard man, and I was afraid you would rob me of what I earned, so I hid your money in the earth and here it is!'**

> **"But his master replied, 'Wicked man! Lazy slave! Since you knew I would demand your profit, you should at least have put my money into the bank so I could have some interest. Take the money from this man and give it to the man with the $10,000. For the man who uses well what he is given shall be given more, and he shall have abundance. But from the man who is unfaithful, even what little responsibility he has shall be taken from him. And throw the useless servant out into outer darkness: there shall be weeping and gnashing of teeth.'"**

> **Matthew 25:24-30 TLB**

The Greek word translated "knew" in this passage is *ginosko*. Its general meaning is "to perceive." (Bromiley, Geoffrey W. *Theological Dictionary of the New Testament* Grand Rapids, MI: William B. Eerdmans Publishing Company, 1985. p. 119ff) A person's teaching, experience and understanding about something or someone shape his perception of that person. So the wicked servant was actually saying, "Based on what I have been taught and what I understand about my master, I perceive him to be a taker not a giver." Perception, even if it is based on erroneous information or misunderstanding, will determine our concept of a thing or person.

The perception of the greater part of the traditional church is based on the teachings of misled ministers who acquired their training in traditional religious institutions. These schools taught their students that God's many outreaches would constantly be in need of financial support. This erroneous teaching has led entire denominations and religious organizations to the subconscious conclusion that God must be in some kind of need, or at best, suffering from a severe cash flow problem. Only the truth of God's Word can set a person free from the mistaken perception that God continually runs His business in some form of financial shortfall.

You must be careful not to base any of your beliefs about God's desire for your financial status on the perceptions of man. You must carefully base every concept you form about God's attitude toward you and your well being, firmly on "thus saith the Word of the Lord." If you don't do this, you will very possibly fall into the trap of organized religion's *poverty doctrine.* Let me give you a verse of Scripture that shows how this kind of deception could come into your life.

> **Poverty and shame shall be to him that *refuseth instruction.* . . .**
>
> **Proverbs 13:18**

## — SACRIFICIAL GIVING —

One of the traditional teachings in the Church is sacrificial giving. It teaches that you must periodically sacrifice, do without, cut back, and limit yourself so that you will have something extra-special to give to God. This erroneous thought process is in full swing in the traditional church of our day. This becomes evident as we hear the professional fundraisers using the following slogan to promote really big giving to today's super-expensive building programs— "not equal giving but equal sacrifice."

For years my wife and I gave in this way. Yes, we gave in faith. However, it was not faith believing for an abundant increase. We gave in faith, believing that if we tightened up on our spending and sacrificed, we would be able to get by without the amount of money we were preparing to give. Please pay close attention. This is not the kind of *faith that brings a financial harvest.* It is nothing more than *faith to be able to get by* on what's leftover, instead of true biblical faith to believe for the harvest proportion increase that God has promised.

You must understand that the faith you exert toward any desired result becomes the raw material that God will use to produce the thing you have asked for.

> **Now faith is the substance [raw material] of things hoped for, the evidence of things not seen.**
>
> **Hebrews 11:1**

Because of this biblical truth, it is of the utmost importance that you give in faith, believing you will receive a multiplied increase of that which you are giving. As my wife and I gave in faith, believing we would be able to get by on less, the faith we used brought forth the frugal lifestyle that we needed for getting by on less. However, that particular kind of faith (raw material) could not bring forth a financial harvest of thirty, sixty, or hundredfold increase. In the same way that the raw material of cotton fibers cannot bring forth a steel beam, so the raw material of getting by on less than before cannot bring forth a harvest of having more than before.

I have heard well-intentioned people say, "I would like to tithe ninety percent of my income." Now in itself, that's a noble thought. It comes from a person who desires to do a good work by tightening up the budget and suffering for Jesus. However, it is also an uninformed thought, for in Christ Jesus, there is a promise of much more than that.

Let's now move to a higher level of understanding and hear the desires of a person who is more attuned to the full potential that exists in Christ Jesus. I have heard properly informed folks say, "I am going to believe God that my tithe will soon become more than the amount I am now earning." This statement comes from the person who has faith to believe God for a harvest proportion increase and the abundance God has promised.

For example, let's say you earn fifty thousand dollars a year. If you are like the first person and perceive your god to be needy, unable to provide any more than you can earn on your own, what will happen? You will have to drastically adjust your lifestyle downwardly so that you will be able to give God forty thousand dollars (90 percent) of your fifty thousand dollar income. In this misinformed spirit of sacrifice, it will be left up to you to find a way to squeeze by on the ten thousand dollars that remain. However, if you perceive God as rich and generous, you will willingly sow your financial seed, expecting a bountiful harvest that will cause you to earn hundreds of thousands of dollars in return. This will allow you to easily give the Lord fifty to sixty thousand dollars a year. Then, true to God's Word, as a good steward you will be able to enjoy the benefits of a forty to fifty thousand dollar increase in your own disposable income. Remember God said that the faithful steward would always be worthy of his hire.

> **. . . the laborer is worthy of his hire. . . .**
>
> **Luke 10:7**

This is exactly what my wife, Pat, and I are now experiencing. It is not that we are living on less, for we are actually living on exceedingly abundantly more than we could have ever even asked or thought (Ephesians 3:20). We now have more to give than we could have imagined possible just a few years ago. We have experienced this increase by faithfully operating the principle of seedtime and harvest in all of our finances. We have done this by moving to a new kind of faith. It's not faith for decreased living expenses, but a much higher faith. It moved us to significantly increase our sowing into God's Kingdom, believing that we would experience a thirty, sixty, or even hundredfold increase from our giving.

All too many of our Lord's precious children are enslaved by the Church's teaching about a needy God. However, in spite of this, there is good news on the horizon. All of this mistaken theology is about to change, for God's Word promises that as the coming of the Lord draws near, a great wave of correction will sweep across the Church.

> **Whom heaven must receive [and retain] until the time for the complete restoration of all that God spoke by the mouth of all His holy prophets for ages past [from the most ancient time in the memory of man].**
>
> **Acts 3:21 Amplified**

The Bible tells us the time has come for God's ultimate desire for His children to come to pass. A great end-time restoration is about to break out across the Church of God. A careful reading of Acts 3:19-21 will show you a promise from God through the Apostle Peter. It is a prophecy that declares that all the errors of organized religious doctrine will be put straight before Jesus returns. Yes, Simon Peter was saying exactly what it sounds like. Restoration is coming and is even now at work in the Church.

## — THE ORIGIN OF THE POVERTY DOCTRINE —

To properly understand the origin of the poverty doctrine, you must be aware of the fact that the doctrinal mindset of the traditional church is founded on a pre-Reformation mentality. The pre-Reformation mentality reasoned that the earthly cathedrals of God must be gold plated and lavishly decorated because they represented heaven on earth. They believed if riches for the believer were delayed until the hereafter, it would be a great motivator to keep people in proper relationship with God and the Church.

However, it only stands to reason that when the world sees the impoverished slaves of this misguided system, they will have to believe their god is poor, or at best, a selfish god who offers nothing more than a religion tailor-made for poor people.

This misconception must be exposed and rejected, for the Church's biblical heritage in no way supports the doctrine of poverty or the lifestyle of poverty. The Bible declares that Christianity finds its spiritual roots in a *very rich* man, for the Bible teaches that our earliest patriarch, Abraham, was extremely rich.

> **. . . Abram was *very rich* in cattle, in silver, and in gold.**
>
> **Genesis 13:2**

Not only was Abraham rich, but the original father of the human race was also rich. Adam was, without a doubt, the richest man that ever lived. He was so rich that he actually had legal control of every asset on planet earth.

> **And God blessed them, and God said unto them, Be fruitful, and multiply, and replenish the earth, and subdue it: and have dominion over the fish of the sea, and over the fowl of the air, and over every living thing that moveth upon the earth.**

> **And God said, Behold, I have given you every herb bearing seed, which is upon the face of all the earth, and every tree, in the which is the fruit of a tree yielding seed; to you it shall be for meat.**
>
> **Genesis 1:28,29**

Upon further examination of our spiritual family tree, you will find that down through the ages, a great number of God's people were wealthy. Let me quickly add that Job was exceedingly wealthy. Not only that, but when God restored him, He did not further deplete his wealth. He actually *doubled it.* Notice that if God had wanted Job to be poor, He could have simply healed him of his festering boils, and left him in poverty.

> **And the Lord turned the captivity of Job, when he prayed for his friends: also the Lord gave Job *twice as much as he had before.***
>
> **Job 42:10**

Isaac is also credited with having a tremendous amount of wealth. His riches were greatly increased by his sowing and reaping. The Bible says he became so rich through the harvest he reaped that the Philistines envied him.

> **Isaac planted crops in that land and the same year reaped a hundredfold, because the Lord blessed him. The man became rich, and his wealth continued to grow until he became very wealthy. He had so many flocks and herds and servants that the Philistines envied him.**
>
> **Genesis 26:12-14 NIV**

The patriarch Jacob also abounded with great wealth. The biblical record tells us he "increased exceedingly."

**And the man increased exceedingly, and had much cattle, and maidservants, and menservants, and camels, and asses.**

**Genesis 30:43**

While the Scriptures do not give us any details about the personal wealth of Joseph, it does describe his great power and influence in the financial and governmental affairs of Egypt, which was the superpower of his day (Genesis 41).

In an open minded and fully informed investigation of the personal wealth of the forefathers of the Judeo-Christian faith, the evidence is overwhelming. The poverty doctrine did not come into the Church through any facts from the biblical record. It had to creep in some other way, that way being the craftiness of the devil and the erroneous doctrines of men.

## — ARE YOU ENSLAVED TO JEHOVAH NEEDY? —

Even as you read these thought-provoking words, you may be realizing you have somehow become trapped in a deadly misperception. In fact, you might be realizing that you are one of those who provides living proof to the world that your god is Jehovah Needy. I want to ask you a very important question, one that has the potential of turning everything around for you and your loved ones: *Would you be willing to change something you believe, even if it went against everything you had previously been taught?* Here's the Bible answer to that question!

**. . . let God be true, but every man a liar. . . ."**

**Romans 3:4**

You may find yourself in the same situation as the one-talent servant of our parable. You may be serving the poor god. You might not even know that you stand in danger of missing out on most of the good things God has planned for you.

**Take therefore the talent from him, and give it unto him which hath ten talents.**

**Matthew 25:28**

You may be asking how this has happened to you. The answer is simple. You have unwittingly been led into the *ruts of the poverty doctrine.* This misconception comes by the false theology of those who serve the poor and needy god, the god who demands that his subjects dutifully fund the projects he so desperately needs. And if that weren't enough, this same poor god also expects you to bail him out of every financial jam he gets into. Here's the truth that cannot be denied:

- **People serving a poor god raise money for him and his projects.** The poor god is the god of the world's religious system. He insists that his servants eke out a meager existence for themselves and his church from the crumbs that fall from the lavishly supplied table of this world's system. They are forced to live with meager resources while being constantly plundered by their self-serving god. They mistakenly believe that this world's flawed financial system is dominant over the financial system of God's Kingdom. They are desperately trying to fund the kingdom of their god out of the dregs that the world leaves for them.

- **The poor god has poor slaves.** The poor god's system of sanctification demands that those who want to be really spiritual must remain poor. They must operate their lives and ministries on the premise of only meeting the most urgent need. They must constantly struggle to acquire that which their religion needs instead of qualifying for God's plan of stewardship that brings exceedingly abundantly more than they can ask.

Once again it becomes obvious that this mistaken, rag-tag band of saints causes the world to conclude that their poor god most definitely needs a name change from Jehovah Jireh to Jehovah Needy.

## — THE GOD YOU PERCEIVE —

By now the alarm bell of good sense should be ringing. Remember that the master in the Parable of the Talents allows his servants the freedom to perceive him as they wish.

**"Then the man who had received the one talent came. "Master,' he said, "I knew that you are a hard man, harvesting where you have not sown and gathering where you have not scattered seed. So I was afraid and went out and hid your talent in the ground. See, here is what belongs to you.'**

**"His master replied, "You wicked, lazy servant! So you knew that I harvest where I have not sown and gather where I have not scattered seed? Well then, you should have put my money on deposit with the bankers, so that when I returned I would have received it back with interest.'"**

**Matthew 25:24-27 NIV**

With his wholly wrong perception, the mistaken servant proved he had learned nothing about his master, even after serving him for years. In his flawed reasoning, he did not perceive his master's real nature; neither did he discern the true heart of his master. Because of this mistaken opinion, he could not project his master's real nature to the world. This fatal error in perception hopelessly locked him into becoming like Satan instead of like the God of heaven, for Satan is the ultimate taker of all takers. Tragically, this inability to properly perceive his master's true nature led this servant into a mentality that caused him to hide his master's money instead of using it in the way his master had intended.

As you continue reading, I will put before you an ongoing stream of proof from God's Word that will give you an undistorted biblical perception of the Almighty God of heaven. From this information, you will become convinced that Jehovah God is the rich God who abundantly gave to Adam, Noah, Abraham, Isaac, Jacob and Joseph. This same rich God also gave staggering amounts of tangible wealth to David and Solomon. He gave incalculable wealth to His Son, Jesus Christ, who stands ready to give to you in such a way that you will want for nothing.

> **. . . we went through fire and through water: but thou broughtest us out into a wealthy place.**
>
> **Psalm 66:12**

Remember these truths:

- The poor god of organized religion is Jehovah Needy. He is the god whose servants must provide for him. The rich God of the Bible is Jehovah Jireh, the God that provides for His children!

- The misguided slaves of a poor god raise money to fund his projects. The rich God of heaven pours out abundant blessings upon his children, who join Him as co-laborers— making His Kingdom on earth as it is in heaven.

- The poor god needs slaves to gather up money for him. The rich God releases money to His children so they can redistribute it for Him.

The choice is simple. Will you serve the poor god, or will you become a joint heir and co-laborer with the *rich God?* I encourage you to *choose this day* to free yourself from the poverty doctrine of this world's religious systems. Become the privileged child of the true and living God who abundantly blesses His children with wealth so that they can be a blessing.

> **. . . I have set before you life and death, blessing and cursing: therefore choose life, that both thou and thy seed may live.**
>
> **Deuteronomy 30:19**

Having established that the God of heaven is the *rich God,* we can now turn our attention to another truth. The *rich God* freely gives us *His rich Son* to save us and help us obtain the abundant life He has purchased for us.

*Our Lord's ministry had such an abundance of funds that even with a treasurer (Judas) who regularly stole from the account, there still remained a sufficient financial surplus.*

# RICH GOD, RICH SON

## CHAPTER 2

Out of the greatest love ever known, our Rich God gave His Rich Son to save, heal, deliver, and restore lost humanity. Everything the first Adam lost and brought to poverty, the second Adam (Jesus) redeemed and is now restoring to the total fullness God promised.

Asserting that Jehovah God is a rich God upsets almost no one. The truth is simply this: God is rich and every thinking person believes that He should be.

**. . . the earth is full of thy riches.**

**Psalms 104:24**

Let me take a moment to give you just a partial list of Jehovah God's immeasurable wealth.

- **God's throne sits in a lavish setting of splendor and fine jewels.** *"And he that sat was to look upon like a jasper and a sardine stone: and there was a rainbow round about the throne, in sight like unto an emerald"* (Revelation 4:3).

- **God possesses the most expensive collection of the purest crystal in the universe.** *"And before the throne there was a sea of glass like unto crystal. . ."* (Revelation 4:6).

— 29 —

- **The city of God is built of the purest of gold.** *"And the building of the wall of it was of jasper: and the city was pure gold. . ."* (Revelation 21:18).

- **The gates of God's city are made of solid pearl.** *"And the twelve gates were twelve pearls: each individual gate was of one pearl. . ."* (Revelation 21:21 NJKV).

- **The streets of His city are made of transparent gold.** *". . . and the street of the city was pure gold, as it were transparent glass"* (Revelation 21:21).

- **God has an immeasurable inventory of possessions including the cattle on a thousand hills, the whole earth and all of its silver and gold** (Psalms 50:10; 24:1 and Haggai 2:8).

- **God wears the finest clothes ever described in human language.** *". . . His train filled the temple"* (Isaiah 6:1).

- **God is the sole owner of the entire universe and all it contains.** *". . . He appointed [Jesus] Heir and lawful Owner of all things. . . . upholding and maintaining and guiding and propelling the universe. . ."* (Hebrews 1:2,3 Amplified).

Now let me ask a simple question:

*Would a rich Father insist that His obedient Son live in poverty?*

The answer would have to be a resounding *no!*

At this very moment in the midst of the Father's infinite riches you will find His Son, Jesus Christ, reigning with Him.

**In many separate revelations [each of which set forth a portion of the Truth] and in different ways God spoke of old to [our] forefathers in and by the prophets.**

[But] in the last of these days He has spoken to us in [the person of a] Son, Whom He appointed *Heir and lawful Owner of all things,* also by and through Whom He created the worlds and the reaches of space and the ages of time [He made, produced, built, operated, and arranged them in order].

He is the sole expression of the glory of God [the Light-being, the out-raying or radiance of the divine], and He is the perfect imprint and very image of [God's] nature, upholding and maintaining and guiding and propelling the universe by His mighty word of power. When he had by offering Himself accomplished our cleansing of sins and riddance of guilt, He sat down at the right hand of the divine Majesty on high.

**Hebrews 1:1-3 Amplified**

## — THE GODLY LIFESTYLE —

So, what is God's lifestyle really like? God walks on streets of pure gold (Revelation 21:21). He dresses His Son with the finest linen suit, topped off with a solid gold girdle.

**. . . in the midst of the seven candlesticks one like unto the Son of man, clothed with a garment down to the foot, and girt about the paps with a golden girdle.**

**Revelation 1:13**

From walls of jasper to oceans of purest crystal, God lives in total opulence.

To demonstrate the acceptable standard of living God expected for mankind, please take into account the significance of the first geographic directions He ever gave to mankind. No sooner were they introduced to the splendid garden in Eden than He gave Adam and Eve detailed directions to the place where they would find the best gold that existed.

**The name of the first is Pison: that is it which compasseth the whole land of Havilah, where there is gold.**

**And the gold of that land is good. . . .**

**Genesis 2:11,12**

Think about the importance of these directions, for God could have given them a map to a number of different locations, some that would have suited the doctrines and traditions of the Church much better. It might have been directions to the holy water, or the baptistery, or even the bathrooms. However, God chose as His first geographic directions to man to show him how to find the finest gold. This is undeniable proof that God's basic intention for Adam and Eve was for them to be rich. There is further proof when you realize that He instructed Moses to build the tabernacle, which was a perfect type of His Son Jesus, of the most costly materials (Exodus 37:15-17). So it only stands to reason that God's Son, Jesus Christ must also be rich, for He is God, and God is rich. However, declaring that Jesus was rich as He walked the rocky paths of the Holy Land really upsets the religious traditionalists. I speak of those who believe the medieval superstition that Jesus came to earth as a poor man, and because of this assumption, they believe His followers should also be poor.

To keep the proper biblical perspective, remember that Jesus was not some poor fellow that God chose to be the leader of the new religion that would be called "Christianity." Jesus is the mighty Son of God who willingly left the realm of glory to tread the earth in search of His fallen creation.

**For the Son of man is come to seek and to save that which was lost.**

**Luke 19:10**

With no biblical basis whatsoever, the deceptive dogma of poverty began to creep into the Church shortly after the resurrection of our Lord. The doctrine of poverty enslaves believers, enabling religious institutions to more easily exploit and control their lives. The devil, under the guise of "penitent poverty," has diverted immense amounts of wealth from the children of God. He has done it through the religious lie that falsely declares to God's Church that poverty is the badge that validates the believer's dedication to God.

In direct contradiction to this lie of the poverty-mongers, Jesus openly declared that His purpose for coming to this earth had nothing to do with bringing poverty, but everything to do with giving mankind *abundant life.*

> **. . . I am come that they might have life, and that they might have it more abundantly.**
>
> **John 10:10**

This wonderful new life in Christ is supposed to be exactly as the writer of Hebrews declared it to be. It consists of greater and better promises than the promises for the pre-Christian saints of days gone by, for we have a much better covenant than they had.

> **. . . he obtained a more excellent ministry, by how much also he is the mediator of a better covenant, which was established upon *better promises.***
>
> **Hebrews 8:6**

These promises bring us into a better standing with God and a much better lifestyle through God.

To receive just a glimpse of the abundance that would have to come with the better promises of our day, let's compare just one of the wealth increases that was received under the old covenant.

> . . . Jehoshaphat stood and said, Hear me, O Judah, and ye inhabitants of Jerusalem; Believe in the LORD your God, so shall ye be established; believe his prophets, so shall ye prosper.
>
> II Chronicles 20:20

This same portion of Scripture goes on to tell us that in that very same day, the Israelites did prosper.

> And when Jehoshaphat and his people came to take away the spoil of them, they found among them in abundance both riches with the dead bodies, and precious jewels, which they stripped off for themselves, more than they could carry away: and *they were three days in gathering of the spoil, it was so much.*
>
> II Chronicles 20:25

In seeing the extravagant way in which these Old Testament saints were blessed, we receive a basis for comparison of just how much greater our financial increase is supposed to be in the better promises of the new covenant of the New Testament.

God's Word says New Testament saints will enjoy even better promises than those of the Old Testament. However, the enemy of our souls (Satan) continues to brainwash religious leaders, causing them to believe and teach that being financially challenged and doing without is somehow a better reward than the Old Testament saints received. They believe this despite the fact that the New Testament gospels totally refute their teaching. Our Lord and His disciples most certainly did not live as vagabonds going about begging their way through Galilee and the cities thereabout.

There is no biblical proof whatsoever that Jesus or any of His disciples ever stood around on the street corner holding up a piece of ancient papyrus with Aramaic words scribbled on it reading, "Will work for food." Rather than this, the Scriptures tell us that

Jesus and His disciples had an abundant supply of everything they needed. They had more than enough to enable them to assemble large gatherings, conduct mass meetings, properly and expeditiously take care of their businesses, as well as running a highly visible ministry. Not only that, but instead of begging for food, the biblical record states that they regularly fed tens of thousands of hungry people.

Please allow the Word of God to renew your mind and transform your finances by helping you discard any and all erroneous traditions or dogmas about the desirability of a lifetime of poverty.

> . . .be not conformed to this world: but be ye transformed by the renewing of your mind, that ye may prove what is that good, and acceptable, and perfect, will of God.

> **Romans 12:2**

Please keep in mind that the children of God are the people of the greater works (John 14:12). Not only that, but we are the recipients of a better covenant and better promises. So let's just believe it, and open ourselves up to the good life that Jesus promised.

## — THE SUBSTANCE OF JESUS' FAMILY —

**And it came to pass in those days, that there went out a decree from Caesar Augustus, that all the world should be taxed.**

**(And this taxing was first made when Cyrenius was governor of Syria.)**

**And all went to be taxed, every one into his own city.**

**And Joseph also went up from Galilee, out of the city of**

Nazareth, into Judaea, unto the city of David, which is called
Bethlehem; (because he was of the house and lineage of David:)

To be taxed with Mary his espoused wife, being great with
child.

And so it was, that, while they were there, the days were
accomplished that she should be delivered.

And she brought forth her firstborn son, and wrapped him in
swaddling clothes, and laid him in a manger; because there was no
room for them in the inn.

Luke 2:1-7

Jesus was not born into a poor family! *Joseph's family had social
standing, material wealth and a solid business.* Let's not forget that
Joseph was summoned to Bethlehem to be taxed. This would not
be required of those who lived in poverty. Not only that, but we
must realize that Joseph was not looking for a barn in which to
spend the night of our Lord's birth. Neither was he looking for a
handout on his visit to Bethlehem. His plan was to rent a room at
the inn. It is a well-established fact that the poor people of Israel in
those days did not rent rooms in the local hotel. Paying for a room
at the inn when traveling was costly. It was the practice of the
wealthy or well-to-do citizens to acquire paid lodging during times
of travel.

It might also cause enlightenment to realize the poor people of
that time traveled on foot. Contrary to this, Joseph provided state-
of-the-art transportation for his young wife. She rode on a donkey.
In addition, the Bible also tells us Joseph had sufficient money to
finance a trip into Egypt that lasted until the death of Herod. After
their extended stay in Egypt, Joseph had enough finances to trans-
port Jesus and Mary back to Nazareth.

Also consider that Jewish tradition dictated that the oldest son receive a double portion of his father's estate as his inheritance (Deuteronomy 21:17). Since we hear nothing about Joseph after the story of Jesus in the Temple at age twelve, most scholars believe, and I agree, that Joseph died before our Lord's public ministry began. This being the case, Jesus would have received the older son's double portion of His father's estate.

You must also keep in mind that Joseph wasn't just some no-name commoner who wandered about in Palestine. He was a direct descendant of the royal lineage of King David. That means He probably had some degree of social status. The Word of God tells us Joseph was a carpenter by trade.

> **Is not this the carpenter's son?. . .**
>
> **Matthew 13:55**

Being a carpenter was a much broader vocational classification in the beginning of the first century than it is today. It indicated that Joseph probably had a construction business. The Greek word that describes his vocation in Matthew 13 is the word for a craftsman in all manner of wood construction.

It is a well-founded belief that Joseph was a man of great integrity.

> **Then Joseph her husband, being a just man. . . .**
>
> **Matthew 1:19**

Therefore, as our Lord's earthly father, he would have projected a clear image of our Heavenly Father's nature to his children. Being a good man, chosen by God to his most responsible position in Mary's life, Joseph would surely have established a good biblical heritage for his children—one that would have been in accordance with the instruction and expectation of God.

**A good man leaveth an inheritance to his children's children. . . .**

**Proverbs 13:22**

In fact, Joseph, as a proper earthly father, no doubt would have given a proper example of His rich Heavenly Father's love to His children. These are but a few of the undeniable proofs that Jesus did not grow up in a poverty-ridden family. There is no biblical proof that Joseph was a poor man.

## — JESUS WASN'T HOMELESS —

Another false assumption made by traditional religious teachers and their followers is that Jesus was homeless. This erroneous superstition is primarily based on a misunderstanding of something Jesus said as He passed through Samaria on His way to Jerusalem.

**And Jesus saith unto him, The foxes have holes, and the birds of the air have nests; but the Son of man hath not where to lay his head.**

**Matthew 8:20**

It is interesting to note that in the context of this portion of Scripture, Jesus was not declaring that He was a vagabond. He clearly states in another portion of Scripture that He had an adequate home where He resided when He wasn't traveling. In the Gospel of John we read about Jesus openly declaring that He had a home.

**And the two disciples heard him speak, and they followed Jesus.**

> Then Jesus turned, and saw them following, and saith unto them, What seek ye? They said unto him, Rabbi, (which is to say, being interpreted, Master,) *where dwellest thou?*
>
> He saith unto them, *Come and see.* They came and saw where he dwelt, *and abode with him that day:* for it was about the tenth hour.
>
> **John 1:37-39**

It is to the shame of organized religion that so many of the precious children of God are living with a mistaken perception of the financial status of the Son of God. This is a major doctrinal error that finds its roots in a total misunderstanding of Matthew 8:20 and Luke 9:58.

> . . . Jesus said unto him, Foxes have holes, and birds of the air have nests; but the Son of man hath not where to lay his head.
>
> **Luke 9:58**

From this isolated part of a much larger discourse, the religionists fabricate the false doctrine that Jesus must have been a homeless person. Now I must confess that outside of its proper context, it does sound as if He were declaring Himself to be homeless. However, when the exact context of our Lord's statement is taken into consideration, it establishes without question that was not what our Lord was saying. This is how the story leading up to our Lord's statement about having no place to lay His head actually goes: Jesus sent an advance ministry team into Samaria to prepare a place for Him and His ministry staff to stay that night. However, Jesus and His disciples were rejected by the inhabitants of Samaria and not allowed to enter the city.

> And it came to pass, when the time was come that he should be received up, he stedfastly set his face to go to Jerusalem,

**And sent messengers before his face: and they went, and entered into a village of the Samaritans, to make ready for him.**

*And they did not receive him,* **because his face was as though he would go to Jerusalem.**

Luke 9:51-53

The reason Jesus made the statement that He had no place to lay His head was not because He was poor and homeless; it was because *the Samaritans would not allow Him to remain in their city that night.*

## — CHRISTIANS ARE NOT COMMISSIONED TO BE POOR —

Let us now turn our attention to another reason for the erroneous teaching that proclaims that our Lord lived in poverty. It comes from a complete misunderstanding of why Jesus instructed His disciples not to take any money as they went forth to minister for Him (Luke 10:4). For some reason, the poor children of the poor god mistakenly perceive themselves as having received these same instructions from their god. They believe they have been given a mandate that requires them to walk in poverty while evangelizing the world.

**Carry neither purse, nor scrip, nor shoes: and salute no man by the way.**

**And into whatsoever house ye enter, first say, Peace be to this house.**

**And if the son of peace be there, your peace shall rest upon it: if not, it shall turn to you again.**

**And in the same house remain, eating and drinking such things as they give: for the laborer is worthy of his hire. Go not from house to house.**

**And into whatsoever city ye enter, and they receive you, eat such things as are set before you:**

**And heal the sick that are therein, and say unto them, The kingdom of God is come nigh unto you.**

**Luke 10:4-9**

As soon as you put all this in its proper context, it immediately becomes clear that on this particular journey, Jesus instructed His disciples not to take any provisions or money with them. He did it because they were going into the "house of a friend" (the lost sheep of the house of Israel). Jewish tradition and etiquette dictated that servants of God would be received as honored guests in the Jewish villages they visited.

As strange as it may seem in light of religious superstitions to the contrary, Jesus never once commanded His New Testament Church to go into the world with this same commission. The Bible tells us that near the end of His earthly walk, *Jesus cancelled this first commission* and completely re-commissioned the Church before sending them into the Gentile world to preach the gospel.

**And he said unto them, When I sent you without purse, and scrip, and shoes, lacked ye any thing? And they said, Nothing.**

**Then said he unto them, *But now,* he that hath a purse, let him take it, and likewise his scrip: and he that hath no sword, let him sell his garment, and buy one.**

**Luke 22:35,36**

Jesus obviously intends for His Church to be well equipped financially for the completion of our assignment. Here is a simple truth about today's world that we all know—it requires money to do just about anything. We need money to secure property, build proper buildings and furnish and equip them for ministry. We need sufficient money to gather the resources necessary to feed the hungry, clothe the naked, visit the prisoner, and supply the needs of widows and orphans.

We also need abundant finances to complete the Great Commission, which commands the Church to go into all the world and preach the gospel.

> **And Jesus came and spake unto them, saying, All power is given unto me in heaven and in earth.**
>
> **Go ye therefore, and teach all nations, baptizing them in the name of the Father, and of the Son, and of the Holy Ghost:**
>
> **Teaching them to observe all things whatsoever I have commanded you: and, lo, I am with you always, even unto the end of the world. Amen.**

> **Matthew 28:18-20**

Everyone knows that airlines rarely allow people to travel at no cost. Automobiles, busses and trucks, as well as the fuel it takes to operate them cost big money. The fact is that we live in a world that requires money to operate. Yes, God does promise miracles; but even with all the miracles, it still takes big money to evangelize the world. If you go to a foreign country and don't speak the language, you will have difficulty conducting any meaningful conversations with the locals. However, if you have the funds to hire an interpreter or to pay tuition at a language school to learn their language, you can communicate the gospel to them. It's a fact that if you don't have a good supply of the currency of the world system, it will be difficult to get much of anything done toward evangelizing the world. Remember the Word of God tells us that "... *money answereth all things*" (Ecclesiastes 10:19).

## — A WELL-FINANCED MINISTRY —

While here on earth, Jesus operated a large ministry with a substantial ministry team—one that needed sufficient funds to meet expenses including feeding thousands of people when necessary. As we have already seen, Jesus had adequate funds to send out advance teams of ministers to arrange for His meetings and the housing of His staff. This is clear from Scripture when you read about His first recorded ministry visit to Samaria. He knew He might not be a welcome guest.

**. . . for the Jews have no dealings with the Samaritans.**

**John 4:9**

Notice the Bible says that Jesus sent an advance team of disciples into the city *to buy food.*

**For his disciples were gone away unto the city to buy meat.**

**John 4:8**

This verse clearly shows that Jesus had adequate finances, for He bought the food He needed for Himself and the many people who traveled with Him.

The Bible also tells us that Jesus used a treasurer.

**. . . Judas had the bag. . . .**

**John 13:29**

Any thinking person knows there is no need for a treasurer unless there are significant enough funds to require a manager. In fact, our Lord's ministry had such an abundance of funds flowing into it that even with a treasurer who regularly stole from the account, there still remained a sufficient financial surplus to keep things operating in good order. The Bible tells us that Judas was regularly stealing funds from the treasury.

> . . . [Judas] was a thief, and had the bag, and bare what was
> put therein.

John 12:6

One more outstanding truth about Jesus and His financial
ethics is revealed to us in the account of the Last Supper. We see
that when Jesus told Judas to quickly do that which he had to do,
the disciples automatically supposed that Judas had been instructed
by the Lord to give money to the poor.

> For some of them thought, because Judas had the bag, that
> Jesus had said unto him, Buy those things that we have need of
> against the feast; or, that he should give something to the poor.

John 13:29

From this verse we see that Jesus was not poor. Instead He
regularly gave to the poor.

## — THE DISCIPLES WERE NOT POOR —

We can also see from this verse that the disciples did not
consider themselves to be poor, for in this discourse they referred
to a group other than themselves as "the poor."

The biblical account states the disciples of our Lord were men
of substance. This becomes obvious when we see the great concern
that arose among them when our Lord gave this warning to those
who were rich.

> . . . Verily I say unto you, That a rich man shall hardly enter
> into the kingdom of heaven.
>
> And again I say unto you, It is easier for a camel to go through

**the eye of a needle, than for a rich man to enter into the kingdom of God.**

**Matthew 19:23,24**

The disciples did not respond to these words in the way that men who live in poverty would respond.

**When his disciples heard it, they were exceedingly amazed, saying, *Who then can be saved?***

**Matthew 19:25**

These men who walked in the inner circle of our Lord show great personal concern, wondering out loud, "If rich people can't be saved, then who can?" Think about it. This response would never in a thousand years have come from the mouths of poor men. Quite to the contrary, if our Lord's disciples were poor, they would have no doubt started rejoicing that poor people such as themselves could easily get to heaven.

The Scripture tells us when Jesus saw their great concern, He immediately began to assure them that all things are possible with God, and even men of wealth could enter the Kingdom of God.

**But Jesus beheld them, and said unto them, With men this is impossible; but with God all things are possible.**

**Matthew 19:26**

Notice carefully how our Lord phrases His response to their alarm. Jesus *beheld them*—not some other group of people—and said *unto them* that with God, even rich men could enter heaven. It is very important to notice that in this same time of concern over their wealth, Jesus makes one of the most powerful promises of abundant increase in the entire Bible or anywhere else. He promises His disciples that everyone who invests their precious things into the gospel will receive in kind a hundredfold increase.

> **. . . every one that hath forsaken houses, or brethren, or sisters, or father, or mother, or wife, or children, or lands, for my name's sake, shall receive an hundredfold, and shall inherit everlasting life.**
>
> **Matthew 19:29**

To get the full impact of this promise, it is necessary to hear it from Mark's account where Jesus said those who give into the gospel would not receive the hundredfold increase after they got to heaven. He was straightforward in declaring that God would fund this promise *here and now on earth, in this present life.*

> **But he shall receive an hundredfold *now in this time,* houses . . . and lands, with persecutions; and in the world to come eternal life.**
>
> **Mark 10:30**

It is obvious from this verse that Jesus really meant it when He said if we give, it will be given back to us good measure, pressed down and running over (Luke 6:38).

The Scriptures give even more proof that the disciples were not paupers, for it is written in the biblical account that their businesses continued to prosper even as they followed Jesus. The Bible clearly states that for a period of time after the resurrection, the disciples returned to Galilee and resumed their businesses, having adequate boats, nets and fishing apparatus awaiting them. They remained so occupied until Jesus commanded them to go to Jerusalem and await the advent of the Holy Spirit. It is also recorded in Holy Writ that the disciples employed *hired servants.*

... when he [Jesus] had gone ... [Jesus] saw James the son
of Zebedee, and John his brother, who also were in the ship
mending their nets.

And straightway he called them: and they left their father
Zebedee in the ship with the *hired servants.* . . .

**Mark 1:19,20**

## — JESUS DRESSED WELL —

While it is not central to the gospel account, nevertheless the
Scripture states that the clothing of our Lord was comparable to
what we would call designer apparel in our day. This becomes
apparent when we observe that the Roman soldiers immediately
recognized the value of his tailor-made coat and refused to divide it
into pieces. Instead they decided to gamble to see who would be
the new owner of this choice garment.

Then the soldiers, when they had crucified Jesus, took his
garments, and made four parts, to every soldier a part; and also
his coat: now the coat was without seam, woven from the top
throughout.

They said therefore among themselves, Let us not rend it, but
cast lots for it, whose it shall be. . . .

**John 19:23,24**

Let me take a brief moment to answer yet another of the
poverty proponents' foolish assertions about the expensive garment
Jesus was wearing. Some people mistakenly assert, without any
biblical foundation, that this splendid garment didn't actually
belong to our Lord. They surmise that such a fine coat could not
possibly be the property of the lowly Jesus. Therefore they render a

wild guess that some sympathetic rich person threw his coat over Jesus to cover His naked body as He labored under the load of the cross on His way to Calvary. Not only is this conjecture without scriptural basis, the Word of God absolutely refutes it, for the Bible states that this valuable garment was His own personal property.

**. . . Let us not rend it, but cast lots for it, whose it shall be that the scripture might be fulfilled, which saith, They parted *my raiment* among them, and for *my vesture* they did cast lots. . . .**

**John 19:24**

It quickly becomes evident to those who demand concise biblical teachings that Jesus would have been a well-dressed man, for He was here on earth as the chief representative of His Father's rich kingdom. He was the most royal of all royal ambassadors that would ever be sent forth from the throne of God. Not only that, but the rich Father that Jesus came to earth to represent is also extremely well dressed.

**In the year that king Uzziah died I saw also the Lord sitting upon a throne, high and lifted up, *and his train filled the temple.***

**Isaiah 6:1**

As the most distinguished representative to visit earth from heaven, Jesus had everything He needed to properly operate His ministry, including the appropriate attire for His royal position. Our Lord's ministry also held numerous mass meetings that included feeding, healing and saving thousands at a time. Jesus also had a staff of disciples (over seventy at times) who had specific responsibilities for making arrangements for the ministry's travel, lodging, food and provisions.

Probably the most compelling Bible proof to absolutely prove that Jesus did not walk the earth in poverty comes from a specific promise God made in the Book of Deuteronomy. In chapter 28, God outlines two totally different standards of living. One is a lifestyle of opulent abundance while the other is a lifestyle of persistent poverty, affliction, and lack.

This chapter is made up of two sections that are concisely divided between verses fourteen and fifteen. The first fourteen verses outline the prosperous lifestyle of those who obey God and live in the way that is pleasing to Him. It tells of blessings so great, they literally overtake those who comply with God's instructions. God promises their livestock and crops will flourish. They will have plenty of provision as well as an abundance to set aside in savings for the future. No enemy will be able to prosper in any attempt to harm them. God also opens the treasures of heaven to them, and they will have the right to live totally debt free. They will have more than enough money to be able to lend to others. The promise is that the obedient ones will have lives that are so bountiful, everyone will refer to them as the head and not the tail.

Now let's take a closer look at the requirements for walking in the promised blessings of these fourteen verses.

> **And it shall come to pass, if thou shalt hearken diligently unto the voice of the LORD thy God, to observe and *to do all his commandments* which I command thee this day, that the LORD thy God *will set thee on high* above all nations of the earth:**

> **And *all these blessings shall come on thee, and overtake thee,* if thou shalt hearken unto the voice of the LORD thy God.**

> **And *thou shalt not go aside* from any of the words which I command thee this day, to the right hand, or to the left, to go after other gods to serve them.**

Deuteronomy 28:1,2,14

Time and space do not allow a thorough explanation of the second part of Deuteronomy 28, which starts with verse 15 and continues through verse 68. However it takes only a brief moment to turn in your Bible to those scriptures and see how those who are disobedient to God's commandments will have to live while here on earth. It speaks of poverty, disease, constant distress, with loss after loss, captivity and despair. God promises this continuing chain of calamity will come upon those who are disobedient to His commands.

> But it shall come to pass, if thou wilt not hearken unto the voice of the LORD thy God, to observe to do all his commandments and his statutes which I command thee this day; that all these curses shall come upon thee, and overtake thee.

Deuteronomy 28:15

The reason for bringing this lengthy discussion about Deuteronomy 28 and its dual promise (one to the obedient and the other to the disobedient) is to ask a simple question: *How did Jesus live His life while He was here on earth?* Did He live in disobedience or in obedience to His Heavenly Father? The Bible answers this question for us.

> And even though Jesus was God's Son, he had to learn from experience what it was like to obey, when obeying meant suffering. *It was after he had proved himself perfect in this experience* that Jesus became the Giver of eternal salvation to all those who obey him.

Hebrews 5:8,9 TLB

The writer of Hebrews concludes that Jesus walked in perfect obedience to God's commandments and instructions. Scripture further proves the total obedience of Jesus, for the Word of God states that Jesus was without sin, proving that He lived in perfect harmony and obedience to God. This record of perfect obedience would have placed Jesus in the prosperous lifestyle that Deuteronomy 28:1-14 promises.

> **For we have not an high priest which cannot be touched with the feeling of our infirmities; but was in all points tempted like as we are, *yet without sin.***
>
> **Hebrews 4:15**

Jesus was totally obedient.

> **And being found in fashion as a man, he humbled himself, and *became obedient* unto death, even the death of the cross.**
>
> **Philippians 2:8**

If Jesus walked in full obedience, as we know He did, every promise in Deuteronomy 28:1-14 would have to be operational in His life. Because of this truth, our Lord's lifestyle would have had to be one of flowing abundance with blessings in the field, in the basket and in His store. According to this promise, He would have to have been a lender and not a borrower, as well as everything else Deuteronomy 28:1-14 promises to those who are obedient to God.

However, if Jesus walked the earth as a poor man as some suppose, it would be the strongest evidence that He lived in disobedience to the commandments of His Heavenly Father (Deuteronomy 28:15-68).

## — THE EARLY CHURCH HAD WEALTH —

As to the biblical account of finances in the early Church, the Scripture tells us the first Church at Jerusalem controlled a large block of financial wealth. The Book of Acts tells us all the believers in Jerusalem sold everything they had and placed the cash in a common treasury. Estimates of the number of church members run anywhere from approximately 11,000 to as high as 20,000. With this many members selling their possessions and laying them down at the feet of the apostles, there were no doubt very large amounts of money in the control of the Church at Jerusalem. This single act of giving created enough ready cash to bless every believer in the Church, properly supplying every requirement that might have arisen.

> . . . with great strength and ability and power the apostles delivered their testimony to the resurrection of the Lord Jesus, and great grace (loving-kindness and favor and goodwill) rested richly upon them all.
>
> *Nor was there a destitute or needy person among them,* for as many as were owners of lands or houses proceeded to sell them, and one by one they brought (gave back) the amount received from the sales
>
> And laid it at the feet of the apostles (special messengers). Then distribution was made according as anyone had need.
>
> **Acts 4:33-35 Amplified**

This is one of the most interesting statements in the Word of God. It declares that the Church at Jerusalem formed a society that was totally void of any lack or poverty. When the apostles had the liberty to freely preach the grace of God and the power of the resurrection, a flood of loving-kindness, favor and good will richly overflowed to every member of the Church. Because of the great liberty in the Church to freely preach the whole counsel of God, there wasn't one destitute or needy person in their midst.

Here, in the special wording of the Amplified Version of this text, we are allowed to see something extraordinary that was taking place. These believers were willing to release their proprietorship and personal ownership of their possessions in favor of establishing biblical stewardships with God.

Notice carefully the words the Holy Spirit chooses. ". . . one by one they brought (gave back) the amount received from the sales" (Acts 4:34). The thing that is the most interesting here is not the temporary communal lifestyle that some people overemphasize. The important thing is that the Holy Ghost says the believers *"gave back"* the amount they received from the sale of these possessions. Now it is evident they did not *give back* the money to the apostles, for the apostles had no prior claim to the properties that were sold. However, God did, for He clearly states throughout His Word that the earth is His property and the fullness of it is also His, that the cattle upon a thousand hills belong to Him as well as all the silver and gold.

Notice carefully that here we see *true stewardship* being declared when former proprietors give back to God that which had been under their control. How quickly poverty, lack and insufficiency would leave the Church of our day if its members would allow this early New Testament mindset of stewardship to once again predominate.

— THE APOSTLE PAUL HAD WEALTH —

As we study wealth in the early Church, it is also interesting to note that the Apostle Paul had money. The Bible tells us he was able to generate enough cash flow that he could forgo taking offerings whenever it was in the best interest of the gospel outreach to do so. The gospel record tells us Paul also had his own business of tent making, a business that brought an ongoing flow of revenue into his ministry (Acts 18:3).

It is also interesting to note that when Paul was in prison under Felix's control, this prominent Roman proctor was after Paul's money. The Bible tells us Felix hoped to get a substantial sum of money from Paul in the form of a bribe.

> **He hoped also that money should have been given him of Paul, that he might loose him: wherefore he sent for him the oftener, and communed with him.**
>
> **Acts 24:26**

Common sense tells us a rich and famous Roman official like the great Felix would not be interested in the apostle's money if it were only a few meager pennies. When considering Felix's interest in bribe money from the Apostle Paul, remember that as a Roman official, he had access to the financial records of Paul and his family.

Add to this knowledge the fact that the Apostle Paul promised in writing to pay all the back wages that a runaway slave named Onesimus owed his master. We read about this in the Book of Philemon. To fully understand the potential size of the debt the apostle pledged to pay, you must realize that according to Roman law, a runaway slave was required to pay his master a day's wage for each day that he was a runaway.

Some secular writers estimate that Onesimus had been a runaway for as many as ten years. This meant he owed approximately ten years of wages to his master. The letter Onesimus carried back to his master contained Paul's personal, handwritten pledge to pay all that Onesimus might owe.

**If he [Onesimus] hath wronged thee, or oweth thee ought, put that on mine account;**

**I Paul have written it with mine own hand, I will repay it. . . .**

**Philemon 1:18,19**

To say the Apostle Paul was poor, you would have to totally ignore all the information in God's Word to the contrary and totally look to the superstition of religious tradition instead.

Now let's address the question that arises from those who would refer to yet another verse out of context.

**I know both how to be abased, and I know how to abound: every where and in all things I am instructed both to be full and to be hungry, both to abound and to suffer need.**

**Philippians 4:12**

There is an easy explanation of this declaration of need that the Apostle Paul makes in this verse. Paul traveled extensively, residing in strange lands and foreign countries for many years at a time. In the day that Paul lived, this kind of extensive traveling would cause him to be physically separated from his material wealth for long periods of time. Add to this the hardship of imprisonment, shipwreck, and the distress of life on the road, and it becomes easy to understand that needs would arise. With this in mind, we see that Paul's declaration of sometimes being in need in no way proves he was a poor man. It was simply a fact of life that came with extensive travel in awkward financial times of the first century AD.

## — HE THAT WAS RICH BECAME POOR —

The material wealth that Jesus either had or did not have is brought into question in the minds of many believers because of a statement the Apostle Paul made about our Lord. In that statement, Paul said that though our Lord was rich, for our sakes He became poor.

> **For ye know the grace of our Lord Jesus Christ, that, though he was rich, yet for your sakes he became poor, that ye through his poverty might be rich.**
>
> **2 Corinthians 8:9**

We can quickly solve the seeming difficulty that arises with this verse by considering two very important things. First, the apostle's statement about Jesus becoming poor can easily be explained by pointing out the difference between the life Jesus lived in heaven and the life He lived while here on earth. Jesus most surely became poor by heaven's standards when He was born in Bethlehem, for in comparison to heaven's riches, He entered a universe of poverty. Leaving that splendid place of opulent wealth to come to the spiritual war zone known as earth could easily explain Paul's statement of Jesus' being rich and becoming poor. However, this in no way proves that He became poor by earth's standards. As we have already seen, He was not born into a poor family. Add to this fact that a number of fabulously rich kings lavishly funded His ministry soon after He was born.

> **. . . when they were come into the house, they saw the young child with Mary his mother, and fell down, and worshipped him: and when they had *opened their treasures,* they presented unto him gifts; gold, and frankincense, and myrrh.**
>
> **Matthew 2:11**

Also notice the biblical record reveals there were a multitude of financial donors who gave generously and regularly into the ongoing operation of our Lord's earthly ministry.

> **And certain women, which had been healed of evil spirits and infirmities, Mary called Magdalene, out of whom went seven devils,**
>
> **And Joanna the wife of Chuza Herod's steward, and Susanna, *and many others,* which ministered unto him of their substance.**
>
> **Luke 8:2,3**

There is another even more compelling Bible proof that clarifies the apostle's statement. This becomes evident when we consider that Jesus not only became poor for us, He also became sin for us.

> **For he hath made him to be sin for us, who knew no sin; that we might be made the righteousness of God in him.**
>
> **2 Corinthians 5:21**

Not only that, but the Scripture also tells us He became sick for us.

> **Surely He has borne our griefs (sicknesses, weaknesses, and distresses) and carried our sorrows and pains [of punishment], yet we [ignorantly] considered Him stricken, smitten, and afflicted by God [as if with leprosy].**
>
> **But He was wounded for our transgressions, He was bruised for our guilt and iniquities; the chastisement [needful to obtain] peace and well-being for us was upon Him, and with the stripes [that wounded] Him we are healed and made whole.**
>
> **Isaiah 53:4,5 Amplified**

These verses tell us of the vicarious substitution the Lord made on behalf of all mankind. In other words, Jesus actually took our place in His atonement by becoming:

- *Sin* for us so that we might be righteous (2 Corinthians 5:21).

- *Sickness* for us so that we might be healthy (Isaiah 53:4,5).

- *Poor* for us so that we might be rich (2 Corinthians 8:9).

Now think about this question for just a moment. Did Jesus walk the earth as a sinner for us? No! He became sin for us at His crucifixion. Did Jesus walk the earth as a sick and diseased man? No! He became sickness for us when He was beaten with many stripes at His crucifixion (1 Peter 2:24).

In that same way, our Lord did not walk the earth in poverty. He became poor for us in His atonement at the time of the crucifixion. The natural outward demonstration of His becoming poor for us was clearly enacted when they crowned Him the king of poverty by placing the *crown of thorns* on His head.

> **And they clothed him with purple, and platted a crown of thorns, and put it about his head.**
>
> **Mark 15:17**

The purple robe they cast about Him was significant, for it represented royalty. But wait! Don't jump to conclusions. These foul jesters were not displaying our Lord as the King of Glory. The purple shroud played only a part in what they were trying to portray. The crown of thorns completed the picture, for that cruel crown was symbolic of the poverty that Adam's sin brought forth into the earth. It is written that thorns and thistles first appeared on the earth when Adam's disobedience loosed poverty into the world.

**And unto Adam he said, Because thou hast hearkened unto the voice of thy wife, and hast eaten of the tree, of which I commanded thee, saying, Thou shalt not eat of it: cursed is the ground for thy sake; in sorrow shalt thou eat of it all the days of thy life;**

***Thorns also and thistles shall it bring forth to thee;* and thou shalt eat the herb of the field;**

**In the sweat of thy face shalt thou eat bread, till thou return unto the ground; for out of it wast thou taken: for dust thou art, and unto dust shalt thou return.s**

**Genesis 3:17-19**

No, Jesus did not walk the earth as a poor man. However, at His crucifixion, as a part of His atonement, He was crowned the King of Poverty. Jesus became poor on the cross.

With this avalanche of biblical proof, it becomes obvious that Jesus did not come into the world to live as a pauper; neither did He minister as a vagabond. Instead, He had abundant finances to do all the Father required of Him as He walked this earth.

Let's quickly review the rich message of promise that Jesus brought from heaven to earth. He promised:

- Abundant life (John 10:10)

- One hundredfold return of houses and land in this time (Mark 10:30)

- An abundant return on your giving (Luke 6:38)

- Answers to your prayers for your every need and desire (Matthew 7:7,8)

The Bible boldly declares:

- God will supply all of your needs (requisitions) in accordance (speaking of quality and abundant supply) with His riches in glory through Christ Jesus. "But my God shall supply all your need *according* to his riches in glory by Christ Jesus" (Philippians 4:19).

- Jesus has made you rich! "For ye know the grace of our Lord Jesus Christ, that, though he was rich, yet for your sakes he became poor [at the atonement], that ye through his poverty might be rich" (2 Corinthians 8:9).

- God is ready to give you more than you can even imagine. "And to know the love of Christ, which passeth knowledge, that ye might be filled with all the fullness of God. Now unto him that is able to do exceeding abundantly above all that we ask or think, according to the power that worketh in us" (Ephesians 3:19,20).

- God already gave you the best when He gave you His Son. How could anyone imagine that He would hold back anything else after giving the best? "He that spared not his own Son, but delivered him up for us all, how shall he not with him also freely give us all things?" (Romans 8:32).

Scripture openly declares that our rich God delights in bestowing riches upon His offspring.

> **. . . let [the children of god] *say continually,* Let the LORD be magnified, which hath pleasure in the prosperity of his servant.**
>
> **Psalm 35:27**

Please notice this verse of Scripture tells us it pleases God when we tell others about the joy He receives by prospering us. In fact, if God's children strictly enacted this verse, we would continually be telling people how much God really wants all of us to prosper. However, in today's atmosphere of traditional religious teaching, you better not say too much about God's desire to prosper His children, or you might be branded a heretic.

It is now time for all believers to take a bold step forward and start totally trusting and believing God's Word as it declares His desire to abundantly supply all of us with all blessings. All we need to do to get started is to drop all of those old traditions of poverty. Then boldly decide to believe all the promises of God without compromise. Just give it a try and see how quickly the biblical promise of prosperity begins to manifest itself in your life.

**Trust in the LORD, and do good; so shalt thou dwell in the land, and verily thou shalt be fed.**

**Delight thyself also in the LORD; and he shall give thee the desires of thine heart.**

***Commit thy way unto the LORD;*** **trust also in him; and he shall bring it to pass.**

**And he shall bring forth thy righteousness as the light, and thy judgment as the noonday.**

**Rest in the LORD, and wait patiently for him: fret not thyself because of him who prospereth in his way, because of the man who bringeth wicked devices to pass.**

**I have been young, and now am old; yet have I not seen the righteous forsaken, nor his seed begging bread.**

**He is ever merciful, and lendeth; and his seed is blessed.**

**Psalm 37:3-7, 25,26**

I invite you to come into full agreement with the things you are learning in this book, and earnestly pray the following prayer.

*"Lord Jesus, I give you praise for the riches you have laid up for me. I thank you for supplying all my needs in accordance with your riches in glory. I claim every one of your rich promises, knowing that you will properly bless me as one of your children, prospering me beyond anything I can even think or ask. By faith, I believe that you will place your desires into my heart and as I commit my ways to you, you will bring every one of those God-given desires to pass so that I may properly glorify you as a faithful steward of your Kingdom. Amen.*

*When you set your heart and mind on becoming a blessing, God removes the blinders, allowing you to see opportunities for advancing His kingdom.*

# RICH GOD, RICH CHILDREN

## CHAPTER 3

**Then said Jesus . . . If ye continue in my word . . . ye shall
know the truth, and the truth [you know] shall make you free.**

**John 8:32,33**

The Bible tells us that the truth you know and are willing to
continue in is the truth that has the power to set you free. Also
keep in mind the truth we learned earlier—*you will always have the
god you perceive.* You can be assured that if you are able to perceive
God as He truly is—a rich and generous God—and if you
continue in that truth, it has the power to set you free from all the
bondage and insufficiency the devil has planned for you. Let's read
it once again, allowing this great Bible truth to become a permanent part of your understanding.

**Then said Jesus . . . If ye *continue* in my word . . . ye shall
*know* the truth, and the truth [you know] shall make you free.**

**John 8:32,33**

## — BEWARE OF COVETOUSNESS —

It's most interesting to note the distinctively different way in
which the properly informed children of the rich God conduct

themselves. They live their lives as stewards and not as those who are sacrificing to fund their God! They know that when Christ Jesus enriches them, it doesn't mean the things God places under their control actually belong to them. They are aware of the fact that no one can legally own that which belongs to someone else.

The Bible irrefutably states that everything on planet earth belongs to God (Psalm 24:1). Not only that, but it is common knowledge that it is covetous to desire to own the things that belong to someone else. The spiritually mature children of the rich God never have a desire to possess the riches He allows them to control. Rather, they consider it a great honor to make themselves available as God's agents. They realize their most privileged position in life is to redistribute God's goods to a lost and dying world. A true steward of God is well aware of the warning Jesus gave every believer to beware of covetousness.

> **And He said unto them, Take heed, and beware of covetousness. . . .**
>
> **Luke 12:15**

Many times covetousness disguises itself in a very deceptive way. It often manifests itself as follows: *"I will tithe and give offerings so that I might become rich and have many possessions to call my own."* While this kind of thought is common among those that hear God's prosperity message, it is totally incompatible with the teachings of God's Word. Jesus teaches a very powerful lesson about the deceptiveness of covetousness in the Book of Luke. There we see the total destruction that covetousness brings to those who allow it to blind them from the truth.

> **And he said unto them, Take heed, and beware of covetousness: for a man's life consisteth not in the abundance of the things**

which he possesseth.

And he spake a parable unto them, saying, The ground of a certain rich man brought forth plentifully:

And he thought within himself, saying, What shall I do, because I have no room where to bestow my fruits?

And he said, This will I do: I will pull down my barns, and build greater; and there will I bestow all my fruits and my goods.

And I will say to my soul, Soul, thou hast much goods laid up for many years; take thine ease, eat, drink, and be merry.

But God said unto him, Thou fool, this night thy soul shall be required of thee: then whose shall those things be, which thou hast provided?

So is he that layeth up treasure for himself, and is not *rich toward God.*

Luke 12:15-21

Let's look more closely at what caused God's displeasure with the rich man of this parable. Our Lord used the words *rich toward God* in describing that which was missing in the man's attitude toward the material goods he had under his control. According to the original language, a much better translation of this phrase would be *"rich for God."* In other words, this man should have considered himself to be *the agent or steward of God.* The foolish farmer of this parable made the terrible mistake of claiming the ownership of things that could never be his. He stubbornly refused to submit to the fact that he could never be more than the steward of the possessions he controlled.

The biggest thing he overlooked was God's purpose for entrusting him with the oversight of the great wealth he had at his disposal. It was the fulfillment of that which God had spoken to

Abraham many years before. He had been blessed of God to be a blessing to others (Genesis 12:1-3). Abraham understood that the wealth God had placed under his control wasn't his to store up strictly for his own personal use. It all belonged to God. He merely entrusted it to Abraham's care for redistribution to all the families of the earth. All too many of God's people are ignorant of the fact that being a blessing to others is a very big part of God's plan for their lives.

> Now the LORD had said unto Abram, Get thee out of thy country, and from thy kindred, and from thy father's house, unto a land that I will shew thee:
>
> And I will make of thee a great nation, and I will bless thee, and make thy name great; *and thou shalt be a blessing.*
>
> . . . And in thee shall all families of the earth be blessed.
>
> Genesis 12:1-3

The foolish farmer of our parable made the terrible mistake of thinking the assets under his control were *his* ground, *his* crops, *his* goods, *his* barns, and *his* lands. He became so totally influenced by the spirit of covetousness that he even presumed his soul to be one of his personal possessions. His mistaken understanding was rooted in a basic misconception of the first great truth of ownership. The fact is that all of the souls of men belong to God.

> Behold, all souls are mine; as the soul of the father, so also the soul of the son is mine. . . .
>
> Ezekiel 18:4

Because of this ongoing series of covetous-driven decisions, God ends up calling this highly favored individual a *fool.*

It is well documented that all the silver and gold, as well as everything else in the universe belong to God. Only a greatly misinformed person would be so foolish as to believe he is the owner of the assets he is allowed to manage. A close examination of God's Word will reveal that God has not called His children to be the owners of their own private hoard of assets. He has called them to be faithful stewards over the assets He places on assignment with them. Once again, we see that when it comes to material things, God's desire is to get wealth *to* His children, not *from* them. The truth is that God wants us to freely use the wealth He entrusts to us for blessing the inhabitants of the earth as well as our loved ones and ourselves.

> **Now the Lord had said unto Abram . . . I will bless thee . . .**
> **and thou shalt *be a blessing*.**
>
> **Genesis 12:2**

## — MORE THAN THE TITHE BELONGS TO GOD —

Many of God's children mistakenly believe that only the tithe of their increase belongs to God. They believe the other ninety percent of everything they can gather up belongs to them. Let's look at how a Christian should mature into a proper understanding of true ownership.

When I was a baby Christian, older saints showed me from the Bible that I should give the tithe to God, so in obedience to God's Word I started tithing. However, as I grew in understanding I realized from Scripture that I wasn't really giving my tithe to God, because the Bible stated the tithe already belonged to God. It was His property, not mine!

> **. . . all the tithe of the land. . . is the LORD'S: it is holy unto**
> **the LORD.**
>
> **Leviticus 27:30,31**

Therefore, it was reasonable to believe that if the tithe belonged to the Lord, I could not give it to Him. So I made the mental adjustment necessary to come in line with the new insight I was receiving from God's Word. With this new understanding, I started returning the tithe to God instead of giving it to Him. Then after a while I came into an even greater understanding of the truth about the ownership of earthly possessions.

> . . . ye have robbed me. But ye say, Wherein have we robbed thee? *In tithes and offerings.*
>
> Malachi 3:8

Then I realized that not only was the Word of God saying the tithe belonged to God, it went even further. This same verse in Malachi was saying that all of my offerings also belonged to God. Malachi 3:8 clearly states that some of God's people were robbing Him, not only of His tithe, but also of *His offerings*. Being that it is impossible to rob someone of that which doesn't belong to him, I had to conclude that if I were robbing God of the offering, the offering must also belong to Him.

Sometime later I grew into an even greater maturity of understanding. I came to realize that not just the tithes and offerings belong to God. Everything that comes under my control already does and always will belong to God!

> The earth is the LORD'S, and the fulness thereof; the world, and they that dwell therein.
>
> Psalms 24:1

This amazing truth immediately brought me to a spiritual crossroads. I had a simple choice to make. I could either rob God by attempting to take ownership of everything that came into my grasp, or I could submit to his lordship and come into compliance with His Word. If I were to be an obedient Christian, I could no longer claim ownership of any material possession. I had to drastically shift my way of thinking and become a steward of the things God put under my control.

Thank God I chose correctly and released my bogus claim of ownership. In that most crucial moment, my wife and I left the foolish ranks of proprietors and became the stewards of the rich God of heaven.

— BELIEVERS MUST LEARN NOT TO GIVE —

This is a very powerful statement that demands an explanation. Yes, I know it might sound like double talk. However, it is nothing more than the orderly progression God has planned for all of His children when it comes to finances and earthly possessions. It is one of the most important parts of growing up in Christ. Let me illustrate. Someone may tell a small child that the stork brought him to his family. However, as a child grows up, he cannot continue to properly advance into maturity with this obviously childish explanation. If he is to be successful in life, he must learn how to put away childish things as well as childish thoughts.

**When I was a child, I spake as a child, I understood as a child, I thought as a child: but when I became a man, I put away childish things.**

**I Corinthians 13:11**

As a mature child of the rich God of heaven, you must learn to stop looking upon offering time as a giving experience. You must start seeing it as it really is, an opportunity to invest and redistribute God's wealth. You must understand that everything God gives into your control is a part of the ongoing blessing you are receiving from Him so that you can *be a blessing to others* (Genesis 12:1-3). That means you must ungrudgingly release to God the right to use any and all of the wealth He places in your hands in whatever way He determines to be proper. It is an unchanging truth that if you try to hold on to the assets under your control, treating them as if they were your own, you will interrupt the flow of God's blessing into your life. Worst of all, you will begin to come under the influence of the spirit of covetousness, which will cause God to call you a fool.

## — YOUR PART IN STEWARDSHIP —

Even though the wealth God places in your hands does not belong to you, you will still be required to make wise decisions as to how you use it. Let me give you an illustration of how this works. Not too long ago, one of our ministry's trucks with a trailer full of books and tapes was stolen. I authorized my son, David, to represent me in the recovery and reactivation of our stolen equipment. My instructions to him were, "David, you make all the necessary decisions, and see to it that we get full value for the money we have to spend." With these instructions, he went to work solving the problem for me. David didn't call even one time to ask, "Dad, what do you want me to do about this or that?" He simply made the best decisions he could to recover and reactivate the truck as quickly and inexpensively as possible.

Soon after speaking to me, the police recovered the truck and trailer. David had the necessary repairs made, and our meeting took place on schedule. He took care of the problem, not because he owned the equipment, but as his father's steward, he took care of things according to my best interest. Most importantly, he did it in a way that he knew would be well pleasing to me. Needless to say, my son is properly rewarded for his work. He receives a good salary and privileges in line with the quality of his stewardship. The more excellent his service as a steward becomes, the better he is compensated.

Jesus taught this same principle in Matthew 25 where the master entrusted his assets to his stewards before leaving on his journey. He left them in complete charge of managing his goods. This parable teaches how the Lord Jesus entrusts us as stewards over His assets. We are to properly manage them and redistribute them in a way that will be of the greatest benefit to His Kingdom!

Let me restate this great truth in the simplest way possible: God desires that you become a *redistribution center for Him.* He wants to develop you into a continual spring of flowing wealth from which He can properly *feed* hungry people, *clothe* naked people, *visit* prisoners, *mend* broken hearts, and send His great message of salvation into every corner of the earth.

— THE IRREFUTABLE TRUTH —

Let's settle the ownership issue once and for all with the following Bible verse as proof.

> **. . . if any man be in Christ, he is a new creature: old things are passed away; behold, all things are become new.**
>
> **2 Corinthians 5:17**

However, let's not stop with the end of that verse. The first part of the next verse completes the thought by saying, "And *all things are of God*" (2 Corinthians 5:18). This literally means that at the time of your salvation when God paid your purchase price with the precious blood of His own Son, everything you had and everything you will ever have became God's property. He has redeemed you lock, stock and barrel.

God has not destined His newborn believers in Christ to become individualists or God-blessed proprietors. Instead, He expects true believers to be spirit-led stewards. It is every believer's God-ordained vocation to be a co-laborer with the Lord Jesus Christ.

— YOU CANNOT LOSE AS A STEWARD —

Jesus tells us the covetous fool of Luke 16 had an insatiable appetite for the ownership of things. His main goal in life was to possess more and more assets. The more the fool had, the more he tried to get. His desire for possessing things was so strong that it finally brought about his ruin, turning him into an utter fool in the sight of God.

The absolute truth of the whole matter is this. Becoming a proper steward will not cause you to lose anything. The exact opposite is true, because it is impossible to lose something that never actually belonged to you. The Bible tells us those who operate properly in relation to the ownership of assets move into a most unique position. They come into the status of having everything, yet not actually owning anything.

> . . . having nothing, and yet possessing [having control of] all things.
>
> 2 Corinthians 6:10

When a person fully understands this truth, he takes on a new mindset that causes him to no longer hoard or hide away assets. The steward's job is that of managing and liberally spreading abroad the ever-increasing store of goods that God perpetually places under his control. It is exactly as the Scripture states:

**There is that scattereth, and yet increaseth; and there is that withholdeth more than is meet [proper], but it tendeth to poverty.**

**Proverbs 11:24**

## — BEING FAITHFUL OVER LITTLE —

Let's look at how God determines the faithfulness of a steward. It is interesting to note that *God does not test a person's stewardship after he comes into abundance! He always tests for faithfulness when a person has little.* Yes, you are reading correctly. God tests your ability to follow His instructions in releasing finances into His kingdom when the funds under your control are the least. The steward that proves to be uncompromisingly obedient when he has very little will soon be trusted with much. Let's see how the Lord Jesus states this truth.

**He that is faithful in that which is least is faithful also in much: and he that is unjust in the least is unjust also in much.**

**Luke 16:10**

Amazing as it may seem, when God calls on one of His seasoned stewards to give a really large amount, He is probably not testing that steward. However, God is almost continually testing the stewardship of the believer that has little, carefully watching for the moment when this steward really loosens up and starts joyfully releasing the exact amount God tells him to release.

I have never met a Christian who was not ready for God to make regular deposits into his bank account. However, *few are willing to allow God to freely and regularly make withdrawals.* If you are going to become one of God's successful stewards, you must allow concepts such as this to become a part of your every day mindset. It is an important part of allowing the mind of Christ to become your mind. Allowing God to freely make any and all withdrawals He desires from your account brings with it the assurance from God's Word that He will steadily make bountiful deposits back into your stewardship account.

> **For God, who gives seed to the farmer to plant, and later on, good crops to harvest and eat, will give you more and more seed to plant and will make it grow so that you can give away more and more fruit from your harvest.**
>
> *Yes, God will give you much so that you can give away much. . . .*
>
> **2 Corinthians 9:10,11 TLB**

— NOT BECOMING HEARTSICK —

It is important that you make constant progress in the success of your stewardship, for the Bible says that going too long without realizing your hopes and desires has the ability to make your heart sick.

> **Hope deferred maketh the heart sick. . . .**
>
> **Proverbs 13:12**

It should be obvious from this verse that you cannot afford to continually hear the message of God's prosperity without experiencing it. The disappointment of never acquiring that which God has promised will cause your heart to become sick. It could even pull you away from the rich God of heaven. This would only further complicate your life by causing you to return to the mistaken doctrines of poverty. Because of this biblical warning of potential heart sickness, all believers should live, give, and believe in such a way that their rich and generous God will be able to abundantly and continually bless them.

Here's an amazing truth. The state or municipality in which you live today understands more about stewardship than the average Christian does.

> **. . . for the children of this world are in their generation wiser than the children of light.**
>
> **Luke 16:8**

For instance, if you were to die tonight, the governing municipality where you live would immediately want to know the name of the new steward of your bank account, your house, your automobile, and all the other assets you thought belonged to you. In the natural realm, no one holds title to any material possession after death. In fact, the greatest degree of legal ownership the governments of this world allow is nothing more than a government-controlled stewardship.

— AN EXPANDED LESSON IN STEWARDSHIP —

Now let's return our attention to what Jesus said about the rich fool and the biblical meaning of stewardship. Please notice the wording of Luke 12:21, *"So is he that layeth up treasure for himself, and is not rich toward God."* This verse serves as the introduction to a body of truth that is completed by our Lord in Mathew 6. By comparing Luke 12:22 with Matthew 6:25, you will see they are both part of the same lesson. Both of these verses, though appearing in different gospels are worded in exactly the same way. *"Therefore I say unto you, Take no thought for your life, what ye shall eat."* We find that when Jesus finished talking about the fool who mistakenly thought the goods under his control were his possessions (Luke 12), He continued this teaching with an expanded discourse. In the continuation of this discourse in Matthew's account, our Lord brings forth detailed instructions of how to operate a proper stewardship.

> **Lay not up for yourselves treasures upon earth, where moth and rust doth corrupt, and where thieves break through and steal:**
>
> **But lay up for yourselves treasures in heaven, where neither moth nor rust doth corrupt, and where thieves do not break through nor steal.**
>
> **For where your treasure is, there will your heart be also.**
>
> **Matthew 6:19-21**

Ask yourself these questions:

- How could you possibly obey these instructions and live a successful life on planet earth? Notice that Jesus says we must not set aside anything for tomorrow.

- Could you survive if you spent every cent and never put aside even one penny for upcoming expenses?

Certainly not! Every successful person must lay up some amount from day to day in order to meet the accumulating monthly costs of living. Knowing this, how could anyone possibly comply with our Lord's instructions to not lay up anything for tomorrow?

My wife and I have learned how to do this, and here's how:

- We don't have a checking account.

- We have no automobiles.

- We don't possess a house.

Now don't misunderstand. We do have the authority to sign on several substantial checking accounts, but those accounts are not ours. They are the checking accounts of the stewardship that God has appointed us to oversee.

The automobiles as well as the home we live in are part of the stewardship we operate for God. They belong to God not us. *There is only one way to live successfully and not lay up any treasures on earth. That is by totally giving over to God any and all assets you now control and becoming His steward.* It is imperative that the true stewards of God look upon the treasures they control as God's property, not theirs.

## — SINGLENESS OF PURPOSE, NOT CONTROL —

Jesus continued this discourse with even more vital information about the operation of a truly successful stewardship.

> **The light of the body is the eye: if therefore thine eye be single, thy whole body shall be full of light.**
>
> **But if thine eye be evil, thy whole body shall be full of darkness. If therefore the light that is in thee be darkness, how great is that darkness!**
>
> **No man can serve two masters: for either he will hate the one, and love the other; or else he will hold to the one, and despise the other. Ye cannot serve God and mammon.**
>
> **Matthew 6:22-24**

Let me illustrate what our Lord is teaching in the following manner. Suppose I own a bakery, and you become one of my stewards. Your assignment is to drive a bread truck selling my bread. You will never be able to be a proper steward for me if you also carry some of your own bread in the back of my truck and attempt to sell it along the way. Here's the problem in a nutshell. You cannot successfully dedicate yourself to my wellbeing while competing with me for your own wellbeing.

The same is true of God's stewards. A proper steward must have a singleness of purpose in carrying out his master's business. As a proper steward, Jesus says you cannot serve both God and mammon.

## — THE MAMMON CULT —

Let's now take a moment and see what is meant by mammon. The ancient Mesopotamians had a mythological god called "Mammon." As they served and supported him, they came up with the concept of lending money at compound interest. From this ancient Mesopotamian beginning, the whole lending industry of this world's system finds its beginnings.

The Mesopotamian people became so prospered by this system of financial increase, they gave up their mythological god, transferring his name to their newfound system of gaining wealth. The present system of commerce based on the practice of lending at interest is, in fact, an expanded form of the ancient Mesopotamian "mammon system."

The entire world system of the lifestyle of debt is totally opposite to the way God wants His children to live. God desires His stewards to be totally free from the mammon system. As long as a steward is tied up by the mammon system, he cannot effectively serve God with the complete singleness of purpose God requires. Satan cleverly employs the mammon system of this world to keep you in the bondage of debt so that God cannot freely make withdrawals from the finances he entrusts to your keeping. When you are in debt, the greater part of the wealth you control will be owed to the anti-God lending system and unavailable to the business of the Kingdom. According to the Bible, those who are in debt cannot fully dedicate themselves as stewards of God, for the Bible says their debt makes them servants of the lender.

> **. . . the borrower is servant to the lender.**
>
> **Proverbs 22:7**

Add to this the fact that Jesus said no servant would be able to properly serve two masters, and you have the reason God wants all His children totally out of debt.

> **No servant can serve two masters: for either he will hate the one, and love the other; or else he will hold to the one, and despise the other. Ye cannot serve God and mammon.**
>
> **Luke 16:13**

Every steward who wishes to properly accomplish God's will with his finances must make a quality decision to get out of debt.[1] Start today by going before your Heavenly Father and renouncing your slavery to the lenders of this world's mammon system. You must also know that Jesus can and does cancel debt. He is also willing and able to supernaturally supply financial blessings that will rapidly release you from the prison house of debt. However, even as you reach out to God for miracle debt cancellations, you must remember that God never releases a financial harvest until you have sown a financial seed. I encourage you to take a bold step forward and start this very day by liberally sowing some of your financial seed into the good ground of a proper gospel ministry. When you do this, you must also specifically believe that as you give to God, He will start working on your behalf to get you rapidly out of debt.

— THE FEELING IS THE SAME —

The Bible says God feels the same about many things as you do.

**For we have not an high priest which cannot be touched with the feelings of our infirmities [our humanity].**

**Hebrews 4:15**

This verse tells us that God senses and feels the things that touch you, and those things have the ability to also touch Him.

When you give to God, He knows your heart-felt attitude and the value you place on your offering. Because of this, He will feel the same way about your offering as you. If your offering is an insignificant amount to you, it will be insignificant to Him. The same is true if the amount you give is very significant to you. God will feel how you feel about it, causing your offering to become very significant to Him.

God's ability to be touched by that which you feel in your heart makes it possible for Him to know when you have given properly. For instance, when the person with billions of dollars gives a million, it seems very significant to those who are observing. However, if it is an insignificant amount to the giver, God senses it, and the million-dollar donation will not be significant to Him either. But let's consider a fifty-dollar gift from a single mother on welfare. Suddenly that fifty dollars becomes tremendously important to God. Why? Because it is such a significant amount to the woman who is giving it. We see this very principle in action when Jesus openly praised the widow who had cast a mere two mites into the treasury.

> **And he looked up, and saw the rich men casting their gifts into the treasury.**
>
> **And he saw also a certain poor widow casting in thither two mites.**
>
> **And he said, Of a truth I say unto you, that this poor widow hath cast in more than they all:**
>
> **For all these have of their abundance cast in unto the offerings of God: but she of her penury hath *cast in all the living that she had.***

> **Luke 21:1-4**

Giving out of your abundance is a godly principle. However, if your gift is to be significant to God, you must not only give out of your abundance, but your offering must be a significant part of the abundance you have! According to these scriptures, we can apply three possible motivations for giving.

- **Wanting to be seen.** Often, people will give large gifts to a ministry or charity in order to be seen. Many times they do so to fulfill a deep desire for recognition from a human source. They like the attention people lavish upon them. It makes them feel important in the public eye for giving a large gift. The folks that give out of this motivation are merely seeking the admiration of men. Jesus said if you give to be seen of men, *you have your reward.*

... whenever you give to the poor, do not blow a trumpet before you, as the hypocrites in the synagogues and in the streets like to do, that they may be recognized and honored and praised by men. Truly I tell you, they have their reward in full already.

Matthew 6:2 Amplified

- **Wanting to be known.** Some people give with a hidden agenda of being known by some leader or powerful person. They place themselves in a favored position by giving into a particular ministry or cause, hoping to bring themselves into association with the person they admire. Without realizing it, they become man pleasers, not God pleasers. Their purpose is to advance their own agenda not God's. Jesus warned about these hidden agendas and once again, after giving, they have their reward (Matthew 6:2).

- **Loving obedience.** This motivation is pure and properly focused. Loving obedience to God is always acceptable. No other agenda or purpose clouds the view of those who give out of obedience to their Heavenly Father. The widow wasn't trying to make a name for herself. She knew that everything she had came from God, and all she needed or wanted would also have to come from Him. When you give a gift in loving obedience to God, it magnifies the size of the gift, causing it to become priceless in the eyes of God.

... Has the Lord as much pleasure in your burnt offerings and sacrifices as in your obedience? Obedience is far better than sacrifice. He is much more interested in your listening to him than in your offering. ...

1 Samuel 15:22 TLB

Giving out of obedience is much more than just giving money. It means that you have an abundance of love and respect for your

Heavenly Father. When you give out of this kind of relationship with God, you will never be tempted to merely "tip" Him. Instead, you will always give that which is precious to you. This is what the widow did, for her love, respect and confidence in God caused her to give all that she had.

**. . . she . . . has put in everything that she had. . . .**

**Mark 12:44 Amplified**

King David emphasized this principle when he said, *"I cannot present burnt offerings to the LORD my God that have cost me nothing"* (2 Samuel 24:24 NLT). The full impact of what David was saying can be realized only when you know the actual meaning of the Hebrew word David used. It is the word the King James writers translated as "cost me nothing." The original Hebrew word is *chen*. The root meaning involves *"the precious."* David actually said he would not give any offering to God that wasn't *precious* to him (David). This principle is of paramount importance in giving. You can be assured upon the power of God's Word that *if your offering is precious to you, it will be precious to God.*

The biblical account of the widow at Zarephath also vividly portrays this truth. The story of her most precious gift to God comes from the Book of 1 Kings. The text tells us she freely gave the prophet Elijah a drink of water, even though the nation was in the midst of a devastating drought. However, when the prophet proceeded to ask her for some food, she refused. She had only enough meal and oil left to make her son's last meal. Notice that the water she gave Elijah was *valuable*. It was probably more valuable than the bread he had requested. However, the bread was *precious* to the widow because it was of great importance to her. It would be her son's last meal.

When she gave Elijah the drink of water, he received it. However, no miraculous increase took place. Not until she gave the thing that was most precious to her did God's hand move to bring the miracle she needed.

> So [Elijah] arose and went to Zarephath. And when he came to the gate of the city, behold, the widow woman was there gathering of sticks: and he called to her, and said, Fetch me, I pray thee, a little water in a vessel, that I may drink.
>
> And as she was going to fetch it, he called to her, and said, Bring me, I pray thee, a morsel of bread in thine hand.
>
> And she said, As the Lord thy God liveth, I have not a cake, but an handful of meal in a barrel, and a little oil in a cruse: and, behold, I am gathering two sticks, that I may go in and dress it for me and my son, that we may eat it, and die.

> 1 Kings 17:10-12

Two obvious things take place in this interaction between the widow and the man of God.

1. This woman is willing to give, for she freely gives of her meager supply of water.

2. She was not willing to give God that which was precious, her son's last meal.

Now catch this next point and all of this will become clear. Elijah knew the cake he asked for would not cancel the good woman's plan for sharing a meal with her son. If she gave it in faith, it would be multiplied back to her. She had given water; so according to God's Word her water supply would be extended. However, if she was to survive the famine, she also needed food. If she wanted to have a multiplication of food, she would have to sow some food.

**Be not deceived; God is not mocked: for whatsoever a man soweth, that shall he also reap.**

**Galatians 6:7**

**And Elijah said unto her, Fear not; go and do as thou hast said: but make me thereof a little cake first, and bring it unto me, and after make for thee and for thy son.**

**For thus saith the Lord God of Israel, The barrel of meal shall not waste, neither shall the cruse of oil fail. . . .**

**1 Kings 17:13,14**

Then true to the word of the man of God, she gave that which was precious, and she and her son had food to eat for many days.

**And she went and did according to the saying of Elijah: and she, and he, and her house, did eat many days.**

**1 Kings 17:15**

Keep in mind that the precious things we give are the things that impress God the most. Are you sometimes guilty of giving God only that which is valuable instead of that which is precious? If so, God will know your inner feelings about your gift. The point I am making is this. God can never look upon something as being precious if it is only valuable to you. Only when you give something that is precious to you does it become precious to God. Remember God always views your gift in the same way you do.

As proper stewards of God, we must be willing for Him to freely make withdrawals from that which is *precious* to us.

## — STEWARDS REDISTRIBUTE GOD'S WEALTH —

From the teaching of God's Word in this chapter, it should become clear that contrary to the opinion of most churchgoers,

God is not calling upon His children to become better givers. Instead, He is calling them to totally abandon the concept of being givers to God. He wants them to become re-distributors for God. The Bible says God's children are blessed to be a blessing.

**And I will make of thee a great nation, and I will bless thee, and make thy name great; and *thou shalt be a blessing*.**

**Genesis 12:2**

To be a blessing you must become aware of the things happening around you that pertain to the Kingdom of God. You must also be ready to take action when God gives you direction. Too often, Christians have spiritual blinders over their eyes that cause them to see only the things that pertain to their own personal desires and wellbeing. When you set your heart and mind on becoming a blessing, God removes the blinders so that you can see all the opportunities around you for advancing His Kingdom. Only then will you be able to see what Jesus sees:

- Poor people in need of a hand up.

- Sick people in need of a healing touch.

- Lonely people in need of comfort and fellowship.

- A dying world in need of eternal life.

As a steward of God's limitless resources, you will have the ability to effectively respond to the needs that surround you in the same way that Jesus did. Remember Jesus said that you would be able to do everything He did and more.

**Verily, verily, I say unto you, He that believeth on me, *the works that I do shall he do also*; and *greater works than these* shall he do; because I go unto my Father.**

**John 14:12**

Do you really think Jesus would make such a promise if He did not intend to give you the ability to fulfill it? This strikes at the very heart of the issue: Do you believe God? Do you really believe that God will place in your hands the abundance you need to fulfill His will for your life?

Most Christians do not fully understand the dynamic plans God has for them. Because of this, they fall short of God's best. They merely eke out a living and give only modest contributions to the work of the Lord. The result is that they never really fulfill God's complete plan for their lives.

It is important to realize that God's highest and best plan for you is that you would be a blessing. In order for this to happen, you will have to have more than enough. It will have to be exceedingly and abundantly *more than enough.* When you have more than enough, you have the ability to meet the needs and desires of all those that God directs you to help.

Now let me help you put this definition to the test in your own life. Ask yourself what the term more than enough really means to you. At first you may think more than enough is an amount that will allow you to comfortably meet your tithe and other monthly obligations with a bit left over. However, God intends for more than enough to be a surplus of abundance, enough for you to liberally bless others as well as yourself. With this kind of thinking, you will immediately start to understand the abundant supply God has set aside for you. Please notice that as your need for surplus increases, God promises to increase your harvest each time you sow!

**. . . cheerful givers are the ones God prizes. God is able to make it up to you by giving you everything you need and more, so**

**that there will not only be enough for your own needs, but plenty
left over to give joyfully to others.**

**2 Corinthians 9:7,8 TLB**

If you operate your stewardship properly, the rich God of
heaven will always underwrite your expenses for doing His will.

— HARVEST NOT MAGIC —

The Bible nowhere promises to increase the believer's finances
by magic. Increase from God always comes to the believer by *seedtime and harvest*. Notice the striking difference that exists between
the stewards of God and those whom God calls "foolish."

- Stewards sow; the foolish hoard.

- Stewards focus on blessing others; the foolish accumulate
  blessings for themselves.

- Stewards shun debt; the foolish embrace debt.

- Stewards are content to be managers of God's assets; the
  foolish strive to manage their own assets.

- Stewards give; the foolish grasp.

The children of the rich God do not release funds into His
Kingdom because God needs their money. Contrary to that, they
know they are ruling and reigning with Christ, reaping generous
harvests from the seed they sow and rich rewards for their faithfulness in handling God's business. Please do not become upset when
I deal with God's many outreaches as if they were businesses, for
Jesus Himself called His work of God a business.

**. . . I must be about my Father's business.**

**Luke 2:49**

## — REWARD MOTIVATION IS GODLY MOTIVATION —

Many Christians become uncomfortable with the idea of being financially rewarded for doing the work of God. Many believers are uninformed if not totally misinformed about *God's reward-based motivational plan.* The truth of this Bible-based plan becomes obvious when you study 1 Samuel 17. A close observation of the facts reveals that at Goliath's entrance into the battlefield, David showed no interest whatsoever in slaying the giant. That is, not until he heard the king was offering a lavish reward for slaying the big bully.

As soon as David heard there was a big prize, he quickly asked for clarification as to how big the reward actually was. *"What will be done for the man who kills this Philistine?"* They told him he would get wealth, the beautiful princess as a wife, as well as living debt free in Israel. Notice carefully that it was only after hearing there was a prize that David decided to fight the giant Goliath.

> **David asked the men standing near him, "What will be done for the man who kills this Philistine and removes this disgrace from Israel? Who is this uncircumcised Philistine that he should defy the armies of the living God?"**
>
> **1 Samuel 17:26 NIV**

In the same way, the Apostle Paul teaches God's reward-based motivation plan when he instructs every believer to run to obtain the prize.

> **Do you not know that in a race all the runners run, but only one gets the prize? Run in such a way as to get the prize.**
>
> **I Corinthians 9:24 NIV**

You can have no doubt about the properness of reward motivation when you realize that Jesus adhered to *God's reward-based motivational plan,* for He was motivated by reward to redeem mankind.

> **. . . for the joy that was set before him [Jesus] endured [the shame of] the cross. . . .**
>
> **Hebrews 12:2**

The Book of Hebrews goes even beyond this in giving irrefutable proof of *God's reward-based motivational plan,* for we find reward motivation to be one of the main biblical requirements for worshipping God.

> **. . . he that cometh to God must believe that He is, and that *he is a rewarder* of them that diligently seek Him.**
>
> **Hebrews 11:6**

There you have it again. *God is not trying to take anything away from His children.* He is trying to get rewards to them. The Bible most truly reveals the living God as Jehovah Jireh, the God who abundantly provides for His children (2 Corinthians 12:14). Let's look once again at irrefutable proof from the Book of Matthew.

> **For the kingdom of heaven is like a man traveling to a far country who called his own servants, and *delivered unto them his goods.***
>
> **Matthew 25:14**

Notice carefully that Jesus didn't say the good master took the goods of his stewards away from them. Instead, he said the rich lord delivered his goods to them, thereby turning them into his rich stewards. The concept of seedtime and harvest was not brought into existence because God desired a gift from His children. Nor does it exist because the pastor, evangelist, prophet, teacher or apostle needs an offering to meet expenses. Seedtime and harvest exists primarily so that God can get fruit (money) to abound to the account of His dear children.

Now, ye Philippians know also, that in the beginning of the gospel, when I departed from Macedonia, no church communicated with me as concerning giving and receiving, but ye only.

For even in Thessalonica ye sent once and again unto my necessity.

*Not because I desire a gift; but I desire fruit that may abound to your account.*

**Philippians 4:15-17**

I encourage you to take a moment and come into agreement with the rich God of heaven by making this declaration with your own lips. God wants to hear you speak it from your own mouth.

*"Almighty God, I confess that you are rich and that you are in need of nothing. I firmly bind myself to you, O Lord, this day as your steward. I am asking you to trust me with just a little, and watch me carefully as I prove myself faithful. I also ask you to break the spirit of debt and poverty off of my life so that I can be free from any and all outward control over the money you entrust to my keeping.*

*"Fill me to overflowing with your Spirit of generosity that I may freely sow into every good-ground ministry according to your direction. Thank you, Master, for abundantly blessing me so that I can be a blessing. I praise you for the privilege of laying up my treasures in heaven, while I am given the honor of redistributing your treasures here on earth. Amen.*

---

[1] If you would like to know more about miraculous debt cancellation and living the debt-free lifestyle, see John Avanzini's books *War on Debt, Rapid Debt Reduction Strategies,* and *God's Debt-Free Guarantee,* and the revolutionary system, The Debt Terminator. To request more information, write to John Avanzini Ministries at the address in the back of this book, or visit your local bookstore.

*Imagine yourself in His presence. How would you describe the massive walls of precious stone, the huge gates of pearl, the streets paved with gold or the vastness of the Creator's throne room?*

# RICH GOD, RICH ENVIRONMENT

## CHAPTER 4

Let's take a moment to think about a canary. I'm talking about the sweet-sounding little bird that sings so beautifully. Without a doubt, only God could create such an exquisite creature. When He created the canary, God carefully crafted him for flying through the air. The canary can be happy only when he is in the environment for which God created him.

With this in mind, let's play a little game with our happy little songbird. Let's pretend we have our little friend in a roomy cage. The cage is placed in a sunny spot where the little canary can sing to its heart's content. Now, let's take that cage with the happy little canary inside, and plunge it under water and leave it there for an hour.

Isn't that a shocking thought? I'm sure it makes you a bit angry. In fact, you must be saying to yourself, "What a horrible thing to do with one of God's little creatures!" Take a moment to think about what caused you to get upset about drowning the little songster. Your reaction is easy to explain, *for everyone knows that placing a creature in an environment that is contrary to its basic nature is morally wrong.* This would also be true if you took harmless little fish, and for no good reason started carelessly throwing them on the bank, watching them flop around, gasping for the water they so desperately needed to sustain life.

In that same way, it would be morally wrong for God to create mankind in His own image, placing His own basic nature inside of them, and then insisting they live in an environment that is totally contrary to the basic nature He has given them.

Let's consider the basic nature God gave to man and the environment in which He chose for him to live. It is of the utmost importance that we remember that God created man in His own image. So it only stands to reason that the proper environment for man would be the exact same environment that would be proper for God.

Now let's consider the rich environment God chooses for Himself.

- God lives in opulent splendor.
- God surrounds Himself with the most precious of gems and costly stones.
- God walks on streets of purest gold.
- God chooses giant pearls to serve as the gates that lead to His City.
- God lavishly uses gold for candlesticks, altars and the many other implements He desires.
- Exquisite crystal extends from His throne for as far as the eye can see.
- His extravagant cape fills the entire throne room where He sits.
- A myriad of magnificent servant creatures waits on His every desire.

This is only a small sampling of the lavish environment it takes to satisfy the basic nature of the God of heaven.

Just try to imagine yourself in His presence. You would no doubt see Him as Isaiah, Ezekiel, John, and Paul saw Him. As you read their descriptions, you realize that earthly language failed them as they attempted to explain the marvelous things they saw. How would you describe streets paved with gold so pure that it was transparent? How would you describe massive walls built with every kind of precious stone? What word could describe twelve huge gates, each one made out of a single gigantic pearl? Just try to imagine the vastness of the throne room of the Creator of the universe. How would you describe the innumerable hosts of heaven engaged in perpetual worship of the rich God of heaven? Try to picture in your imagination a sea of purest crystal without one spot or blemish, magnificent glassware that stretches as far as the eye can see. What words would you use to describe a crystal-clear, living river that flows continuously out of the great city of God? What adjective would you employ to describe the majestic trees of life that flourish on each side of the river, trees that perpetually bring forth miracle fruit that has the power to heal the nations?

As you picture this glorious sight, could you imagine the rich God of heaven living in anything less than this opulent splendor?

Now try to imagine how the heart of God must grieve when He sees His blood-bought children—those He declares to be bone of His bone and flesh of His flesh. Think of how He must feel, seeing His beloved children living in a world polluted by sin, sickness, and sorrow, while His living conditions are lush and untainted. Imagine His heartache as His Bride, the Church, struggles in poverty and insufficiency. Please notice that anything that pertains to these conditions of lack and poverty is absolutely contrary to the nature He placed within the creature He called "mankind." Keep in mind that in the midst of this contradiction of contradictions, those that know God best refer to Him as Jehovah Jireh, the God Who Provides for His children.

## — THE PERFECT ENVIRONMENT FOR MANKIND —

Now with this picture still fresh in your mind, allow your spirit man to take hold of the next thing you are going to read. When God created mankind, He placed within him the same extravagant nature that He has within Himself.

> **And God said, Let us make man in our image, after our likeness: and let them have dominion over the fish of the sea, and over the fowl of the air, and over the cattle, and over all the earth, and over every creeping thing that creepeth upon the earth.**
>
> **So God created man** *in his own image,* **in the image of God created he him; male and female created he them.**
>
> **Genesis 1:26,27**

Lest you make the mistake of believing that since the fall of Adam, the divine nature of God no longer resides within mankind, I point out that while fallen mankind did lose the divine nature, God freely restores it to everyone who is born again.

> **Whereby are given unto us exceeding great and precious promises: that by these** *ye might be partakers of the divine nature,* **having escaped the corruption that is in the world through lust.**
>
> **2 Peter 1:4**

Add to this knowledge an even greater understanding of the

opulent garden that God created for mankind, for when God made a dwelling place for man, He placed him in the exact same place that He designed for Himself. It is important that you realize that God put Adam and Eve in Eden. Notice the Bible doesn't say God placed Adam in the Garden of Eden. He put him in a garden in Eden.

> **And the LORD God planted a garden eastward *in* Eden; and there he put the man whom he had formed.**
>
> **Genesis 2:8**

## — EDEN—THE PARADISE OF GOD —

To see the real significance of this information, I must show you a bit more about what the word *Eden* really means. In its original form, it is the word *Aden*. Aden literally means "the place of *voluptuous pleasures.*" It was a place that was perfectly pleasing and satisfying to the basic nature of God as well as to His duplicate nature—the nature He placed in the new species He made in His own image. To find the location of this most splendid place called "Eden," it is necessary to go to the New Testament and study the parallel Greek word for Eden, which is *paradeios*. It is pronounced *paradise* in English.

Paradise is mentioned only three times in the New Testament.

- Jesus spoke of Paradise on the cross when he told the repentant thief, *"I tell you the truth, today you will be with me in **paradise"*** (Luke 23:43 NIV).

- Paul wrote about a man (probably himself) caught up into the third heaven, which was called ***Paradise*** (2 Corinthians 12:2-4).

- Revelation 2:7 also mentions Paradise when the Lord says, *"To him who overcomes, I will give the right to eat from the tree of life, which is in the **paradise** of God"* (NIV).

Here we gain valuable insight about Eden (paradise). It is broadly believed that Jesus is the Tree of Life. This passage tells us the Tree of Life (Jesus) is located in the midst of the *paradise of God.* If paradise is the place where Jesus resides, it also has to be *the place where God resides,* for Jesus and God are one.

Now hold on to your hat, for the next thought totally destroys any possibility that God would want any of His children living in poverty. If God has put His own extravagant, opulent, rich nature inside His children, it would be totally wrong for Him to insist that His sons and daughters live in an environment other than that which would be suitable for Him. If Eden properly suited God's divine nature, then only a garden in Eden would be suitable for Adam and Eve whom He created in His own image, placing in them His own basic nature.

Think for a moment of the care God lavished on the garden He planted in Eden prior to Adam and Eve's occupation of it. The diminished lifestyle of the Church today would be as filthy rags compared to the beauty of the garden in paradise. Yes, Eden was like heaven itself.

Notice that God created each species with a distinctive nature. Then He lovingly placed them in the environment best suited for that nature. Remember our canary. He could be happy only in the environment God created for him. This is true of all God's living creatures.

Now to keep from making the same mistake the children of the poor god make, it is important that you remember the high quality of the basic nature God has placed inside you. It is exactly the same as His nature. Therefore, it will never be possible for you to be truly content until you reside in an environment like your Creator's. Remember that after placing the birds in the sky, the fish in the seas, and the beasts in the grassy fields, God placed mankind in an opulent garden in the same place He dwelled.

> **Now the Lord God had planted a garden in the east, in Eden; and there he put the man he had formed. And the Lord God made all kinds of trees grow out of the ground—trees that were pleasing to the eye and good for food. In the middle of the garden were the tree of life and the tree of the knowledge of good and evil.**
>
> **A river watering the garden flowed from Eden, and from there it divided; it had four headstreams. The name of the first is the Pishon; it winds through the entire land of Havilah, where there is gold. (The gold of that land is good; aromatic resin and onyx are also there.)**
>
> **Genesis 2:8-12 NIV**

Listen carefully to the language the Word of God uses when it describes the opulence of Eden. Every tree was pleasant to the sight. There was an abundance of everything good to eat. Not only that, but close at hand were gold and precious stones. Everything in Eden was exactly the way God liked it. Scripture says God looked upon all that He had created and pronounced that it was good and acceptable to Him. Because of this, God knew it would be exactly the way Adam and Eve would want it, for the garden was exactly the way God Himself would want it to be.

— LIVING WITH GOD IN PARADISE —

Realizing that Paradise is the exact environment God chooses for Himself, it is only proper that He would have man live there with Him. This heartfelt desire of God to have mankind live in abundant blessings and the most desirable of circumstances appears throughout Scripture. As amazing as it may seem, God's first words to mankind were a command to infinitely increase the opulence they were already enjoying. Hear the abundant richness of the first words God ever spoke to man. "You can have more." In their first face-to-face conversation, God told Adam He wanted Him to have many times more than he already had.

**And God blessed them [enabled them to prosper], and God said unto them, Be fruitful, and multiply. . . .**

**Genesis 1:28**

In other words, God told Adam He desired for him to have thirty times more, sixty times more, and even a *hundred times* more.

— THE DEVIL WANTS TO STEAL YOUR INHERITANCE —

Now catch the striking contrast of purpose between God's desire for mankind and the devil's desire for them. Satan's first words to Adam offered only hard work with no hope of reward.

**Now the serpent was more crafty than any of the wild animals the Lord God had made. He said to the woman, "Did God really say, "You must not eat from any tree in the garden'?"**

**Genesis 3:1-2 NIV**

Notice carefully that the devil's first words to mankind were a direct contradiction of God's promise of ever-increasing prosperity. Now get this basic truth firmly implanted into your thinking. The Bible proves *the devil is the father of the poverty doctrine,* for it records that Satan was the first one to ever proclaim the dismal doctrine of poverty and insufficiency.

. . . "Did God really say, 'You must not eat from any tree in the
garden'?"

**Genesis 3:1 NIV**

This is the exact opposite of what God originally said to Adam
when He released to him the oversight of the beautiful garden in
Eden.

. . . "You are free to eat from any tree in the garden. . . ."

**Genesis 2:16 NIV**

The devil's deepest desire is for mankind to be poverty-stricken,
living a life of despair, for he knows the environment of lack and
insufficiency is totally incompatible to the nature of God. Envy of
man and his God-given nature, the nature that makes man like
God Jehovah, was the driving force that brought Satan into dis-
harmony and total rebellion.

You said in your heart, "I will ascend to heaven; I will raise
my throne above the stars of God; I will sit enthroned on the
mount of assembly, on the utmost heights of the sacred mountain.

"I will ascend above the tops of the clouds; *I will make myself
like the Most High.*"

**Isaiah 14:13,14 NIV**

Because of this envy, God has cursed the devil's path with an
unchangeable destiny of separation from God and His children.

So the Lord God said to the serpent, "Because you have done
this, Cursed are you above all the livestock and all the wild
animals! You will crawl on your belly and you will eat dust all the
days of your life."

**Genesis 3:14 NIV**

With Adam and Eve's rebellion, thorns and thistles immediately began to grow in place of the bountiful produce to which

they had become accustomed. With the fall, everything in the future of all humanity changed. Yes, we have beautiful vistas of grandeur here on earth. Yes! There are places on this planet that seem to take our breath away with their awesome beauty. However, all this beauty is temporal, for it will all be destroyed in a cataclysmic moment of time.

Lest we forget the high position of power and authority from which Satan (Lucifer) fell, let the Word of God remind us of his former position.

> **How art thou fallen from heaven, O Lucifer, son of the morning! how art thou cut down to the ground, which didst weaken the nations!**
>
> **For thou hast said in thine heart, I will ascend into heaven, I will exalt my throne above the stars of God: I will sit also upon the mount of the congregation, in the sides of the north:**
>
> **I will ascend above the heights of the clouds; I will be like the most High.**
>
> **Yet thou shalt be brought down to hell, to the sides of the pit.**
>
> **Isaiah 14:12-15**

After falling from his position of favor, Satan became possessed with hatred for God and everything that was important to God. Of course, this turned him totally against mankind, and especially against that portion of the human race that would make Jehovah their God.

— GOD DESIGNED EDEN FOR HIMSELF AND MAN —

God created a garden in Eden, a place where God and man could dwell together. I believe you can now see how immoral it would be for God to insist that His children be permanently banished from the environment that He created for them. The truth is that God placed man in the garden in Eden with a prime directive to make it even more prosperous and splendid than it was when He placed it in Adam's care. Redeemed mankind's proper place is alongside God, joined with Him in a splendid, ever-increasing coexistence.

When God created Eden, He made it complete. The garden lacked nothing, because everything that would satisfy God's own nature was there. The very fact that God chose the garden for Adam implies that nothing necessary for Adam's peace and satisfaction was missing. In fact, Scripture tells us Adam's God-given task was to dress and keep the garden. This tells us the garden in Eden was already producing bountifully when Adam arrived on the scene. Here's the good news. Adam and Eve didn't have to start from scratch. God gave them a divine jumpstart by providing them with everything their divine nature could desire. The simple truth is that the rich God of heaven started them out as rich and prosperous stewards of the voluptuous garden in Eden.

How awesome it is to realize that God loved them so much that *He didn't require them to start at the bottom* and work their way up. God elevated them to royal status from the very beginning of their existence. That is exactly the same way God starts out every new convert. They start out as joint-heirs with Christ Jesus.

The result of the curse that came upon Adam and Eve when they disobeyed was much more devastating than mere banishment from the garden to toil and sweat for their living. It was the penalty of spiritual blindness, for they were no longer able to freely come and go from God's presence. Their greatly treasured daily visits with Him were abruptly brought to an end.

## — BACK TO EDEN —

Everyone who properly understands the redemptive work of Jesus Christ knows He has redeemed and restored mankind's right to dwell in God's rich environment. He graciously did this so that all of God's children could enjoy an ever-increasing, never-ending abundant relationship with God. Through the redemptive work of His Son, God graciously provided a way for mankind to re-enter the flourishing lifestyle of Eden.

> **For ye know the grace of our Lord Jesus Christ, that, though he was rich, yet for your sakes he became poor, that ye through his poverty might be rich.**
>
> **2 Corinthians 8:9**

Jesus proved His desire to restore man to the opulence of paradise when He pronounced His all-inclusive invitation to the thief on the cross.

> **. . . today you will be with me in paradise.**
>
> **Luke 23:43 NIV**

At Calvary, Jesus paid the full price, and God wrote the invitation in His Son's own blood, an invitation to all of mankind to come back with Him to paradise where they belong. Because of our Lord's death on the cross, all those who will may come back to the environment that is completely compatible with their new nature in Christ Jesus.

God is calling for us to pick up our relationship with Him where our ancient ancestors left off, once again joining Him in experiencing His limitless riches. The death of Christ on the cross of Calvary has brought us back to square one where God is telling all believers they can have much more than they now have. He who has an ear to hear, listen to God's Word and you will hear Him personally invite you to once again "be fruitful and multiply." My personal prayer is that you will say yes to God's gracious invitation to return to the splendid Eden-like life God has planned for you.

> **. . . the Spirit and the bride say, Come. And let him that heareth say, Come. And let him that is athirst come. And whosoever will, let him take the water of life freely.**
>
> **Revelation 22:17**

## — ARE YOU LIVING IN EDEN? —

When Adam and Eve rebelled against God, death entered the creation. Mankind died spiritually as well as physically. Sin began to darken their souls, and the rest of creation also began to suffer the consequences of their disobedience (Romans 8:19 21). The horrible death Adam and Eve suffered is directly tied to the poverty message the devil brought to them in the garden in Eden. The devil lied by telling them God would withhold from them the good life He had promised.

> **". . . Did God really say, "You must not eat from any tree in the garden'?"**
>
> **Genesis 3:1 NIV**

So with this oldest of deceptions, Satan enticed God's creation to disobey His command, plunging the whole human race into separation from the God that created them.

The hard truth is that when Adam and Eve sinned, they exposed themselves to a curse. It is important that you understand that if you're not living under God's covering, you are living under a curse; there is no in-between. You are either dominant through

Christ Jesus, or you are being dominated by Satan. With Adam's rebellion, the ground under his feet began to bring forth thorns and thistles. This caused Adam to have to earn his living by the sweat of his brow. This new status that came with the fall is a stark contrast to the splendid life he was entitled to have before he rebelled.

Exposure to this curse has steadily continued from that day to this, for the greater part of humanity still has to expend a great amount of labor, sweat and tears to eke out a living from this present world system. However, there is *good news!* Just as mankind's sin exposed him to the curse, God stands ready to once again cover mankind when they come into agreement with His provision for their salvation through Christ Jesus. When we become the born-again children of the King of Kings, He elevates us to an even greater status than mankind enjoyed before the fall. At the new birth, redeemed mankind no longer lives with God as a created being. He now has the exalted privilege to live with God as His son or daughter.

Thank God the truth of His Word breaks every curse and exposes every lie of the devil. Here are a few simple questions that will help you determine if your present lifestyle is truly compatible with the divine nature that God has given you.

- Are you living under a blessing or a curse?

- Are you prosperous or needy?

- Are you experiencing increase or constant shortage?

- Are you sowing and reaping abundant harvests or are you constantly forced to eat your seed?

- Are you free or bound?

- Are you dominant or dominated?

- Are you walking in abounding health or diminishing health?

- Are you projecting yourself to the world as the rich child of the rich God of heaven or as the impoverished servant of a poor god?

## — THE POOR GOD SEEKS YOUR INHERITANCE —

The slaves of Jehovah Needy are systematically signing over their rightful inheritance to a greedy, selfish god. Their lot in life is to be incomplete, dissatisfied, hopeless, depressed, and no more than average at best. They have no vision of a prosperous future because their eyes are constantly turned downward, searching for the crumbs that fall from the rich man's table. Their selfless worship of their poor god fills them with an unspoken but nevertheless morbid dread of their financial future. While they seek ways to merely get by, the lost people of this world shake their heads in disbelief, wondering why anyone would want to serve a god like that?

As hopeless as their entrapment may seem, there is a way of escape. Yes, Jesus Christ has provided an *Emancipation Proclamation*. It comes directly from the realm of glory! He is the executor of a New Covenant that promises a bright future for those who have lost their way. Jesus has come to set the captives free and release them from their service to the poor, greedy god that gobbles up every cent they have with each passing of the offering plate.

This is the perfect day for you to tap into the reservoir of the rich God's abundance and drink deeply of the life-saving water that's available to all God's children. Yes, God will help you return from the path of financial disaster and redirect you toward the prosperity the Scripture promises. Today, you are eligible to receive from God all the rich promises of His Word. All you have to do is look up and freely receive the wonderful things God is trying to deliver to you.

As you no doubt know, the enemy will always try to remind you of where you've been. You may feel as though you have no future. However, never forget that only God knows the full glory and abundance He has set aside for you. Just think about it. If He created such splendor for Adam and Eve, you know that you, as His blood-bought child, have even better things waiting for you. Now that you know the truth, you must reach out and grab hold of it.

— LET THE TRUTH OF GOD OPEN YOUR EYES —

Let's compare what the poor god of religious tradition and the rich God really want for you.

- THE RICH GOD OF HEAVEN WANTS YOU TO BE HEALTHY AND ABOUNDING IN HIS RICHES.

- The poor god wants you to be sickly, with one foot moving steadily toward the grave and the other pointed in the direction of the bankruptcy court.

- THE RICH GOD OF HEAVEN WANTS YOU TO BE A SUCCESS.

- The poor god wants you to fall into mediocrity, always abiding under the heel of unscrupulous men.

- THE RICH GOD OF HEAVEN WANTS EVERYTHING YOUR HAND TOUCHES TO PROSPER.

- The poor god wants everything your hand touches to eventually be sacrificed to him in the offering plate.

The truth is your new birth in Christ has equipped you with everything you need to produce the abundant life God has reserved for you. Just think about it a moment and you will see how great your advantage in life really is, for your God has given you the mind of Christ. Our Lord's wisdom is yours for the taking. Your God's abilities and gifts flow to you from the Holy Ghost (1 Corinthians, chapters 12-14).

> **Then Peter said unto them, Repent, and be baptized every one of you in the name of Jesus Christ for the remission of sins, and ye shall receive the gift of the Holy Ghost.**
>
> **Acts 2:38**

Your previous environment and circumstances can no longer keep you from prospering. You are a citizen in good standing of God's opulent Kingdom of Light. You are not at the brink of bankruptcy. You stand at the threshold of the wide-open doors of streaming prosperity! All you have to do is ask, seek and knock, and it's yours.

> **Ask, and it shall be given you; seek, and ye shall find; knock, and it shall be opened unto you.**
>
> **Matthew 7:7**

I encourage you to drop the poor god of the religionists like a hot rock and boldly stake your claim to the rich environment that God has purchased for you.

> **And it shall come to pass, if thou shalt hearken diligently unto the voice of the LORD thy God, to observe and to do all his**

commandments which I command thee this day, that the LORD thy God will set thee on high above all nations of the earth:

And *all these blessings shall* come on thee, and *overtake thee,* if thou shalt hearken unto the voice of the LORD thy God.

Blessed shalt thou be in the city, and blessed shalt thou be in the field.

Blessed shall be the fruit of thy body, and the fruit of thy ground, and the fruit of thy cattle, the increase of thy kine, and the flocks of thy sheep.

Blessed shall be thy basket and thy store.

Blessed shalt thou be when thou comest in, and blessed shalt thou be when thou goest out.

The LORD shall cause thine enemies that rise up against thee to be smitten before thy face: they shall come out against thee one way, and flee before thee seven ways.

The LORD shall command the blessing upon thee in thy store-houses, and in all that thou settest thine hand unto; and he shall bless thee in the land which the LORD thy God giveth thee.

The LORD shall establish thee an holy people unto himself, as he hath sworn unto thee, if thou shalt keep the commandments of the LORD thy God, and walk in his ways.

And all people of the earth shall see that thou art called by the name of the LORD; and they shall be afraid of thee.

And the LORD shall make thee plenteous in goods, in the fruit of thy body, and in the fruit of thy cattle, and in the fruit of thy ground, in the land which the LORD sware unto thy fathers to give thee.

The LORD shall open unto thee his good treasure, the heaven to give the rain unto thy land in his season, and to bless all the work of thine hand: and thou shalt lend unto many nations, and thou shalt not borrow.

*And the LORD shall make thee the head, and not the tail; and thou shalt be above only, and thou shalt not be beneath; if that thou hearken unto the commandments of the LORD thy God, which I command thee this day, to observe and to do them:*

And thou shalt not go aside from any of the words which I command thee this day, to the right hand, or to the left, to go after other gods to serve them.

**Deuteronomy 28:1-14**

All these promises belong to the obedient believer! Reach out and take hold of that which is rightfully yours. God wants to set you on high and bring all of these blessings into your life. Go back over these fourteen verses and you will see that God wants you:

- Blessed in the city and in the field

- Fruitful in your body

- Abounding in the production of your fields

- Abounding in the increase of your flocks and herds

- Abounding in the bounty of your basket (your daily supply)

- Abounding in your storehouses (your savings accounts)

- Victorious over all your enemies, causing those who come against you from one direction to flee from you in seven directions

- Successful in everything you set your hand to do

- Known throughout the land by the name of the Lord

- Abounding in the treasures of heaven

- Lending your money but not having to borrow

- Ruling in life as the head and not the tail-end of humanity

- Always coming out above, never ending up underneath

You are a chosen child of the King of Glory. You are eligible to receive all that God has. He graciously invites you into the store-house of heaven. Not only will God meet your needs; He will abundantly bless you so that you can be a blessing to others. He invites you to become a co-laborer with Jesus Christ, eliminating need, pain, hunger, and ignorance from the masses of this earth. Jehovah Jireh has made a solemn promise to be your provider, not your plunderer.

*Stewards move into a most unique position. They come into the status of having everything, while actually owning nothing.*

# RICH CHILDREN ENJOY THE RICHES OF HIS GLORY

## CHAPTER 5

At the beginning of this book, I set the scene of a rich father having a poor child. If a rich father has a poor child, we might assume one of the following:

1. The father is not loving and caring. So, the father doesn't provide for the needs of his child.

2. The father is loving and caring, but for some reason the child refuses to accept the father's provisions.

Let's bury any notion that the first point is true about our Heavenly Father. Every person who knows anything about the rich God of heaven knows He is loving and caring. He is a God who is concerned about every need and desire of His children. We know He loves us because He has already given us the most valuable thing He has.

> **Even if we were good, we really wouldn't expect anyone to die for us, though, of course, that might be barely possible. But God showed his great love for us by sending Christ to die for us while we were still sinners. And since by his blood he did all this for us as sinners, how much more will he do for us now that he has declared us not guilty? . . .**
>
> **Romans 5:7-9 TLB**

Not only that, but God's Word goes even further and tells us it is pleasing to God when His children prosper.

> . . . **Let the LORD be magnified, which hath pleasure in the prosperity of his servant.**
>
> Psalms 35:27

Even beyond that, the Scripture says God has given each of His children *supernatural power to accumulate wealth.*

> **But thou shalt remember the LORD thy God: for it is he that giveth thee power to get wealth. . . .**
>
> Deuteronomy 8:18

God backs up this statement with an explanation of how His children get this supernatural empowerment to prosper.

> **The blessing [supernatural empowerment to prosper] of the Lord brings wealth, and he adds no trouble to it.**
>
> Proverbs 10:22 NIV

Notice that when the Word of God speaks of blessings, it primarily speaks of things or benefits. However, when it speaks of the *blessing of God,* it primarily speaks of a divine empowerment. It is evident from these verses and many other scriptures that it is the perfect will of our Heavenly Father to abundantly bless all His children. He does this so they will be able to fully enjoy the many benefits that flow from the divine empowerment to prosper that He has given them. However, even with this wonderful promise of supernatural enabling, there are many unproductive habits, excesses, and unscriptural thought patterns that hinder the majority of believers from the rich benefits that come with being a child of God. The roadblocks to God's best are many. Here are just a few.

- *Misinformation.* You may have received wrong information that led you to believe that it's immaterial to God whether you are rich or poor.

- *Ignorance.* You may not have been exposed to the wonderful things the Bible says about God's desire for your financial success.

- *Laziness.* You may not be fully using the skills, gifts, knowledge and creativity God has given you for bringing forth the prosperous lifestyle He has promised.

- *Misperception.* Through misguided teaching and preaching, you may perceive God as a greedy taker instead of a generous giver.

- *False doctrine.* Your religious upbringing may have taught you that poverty is a badge of goodness, honesty, and godliness, causing you to believe God wants you to be poor.

— GOD'S GLORY —

There is a powerful process working in every believer. It is an unseen power that is either drawing you into God's best or guiding you farther from it. When you are sincerely believing God's Word and trying your best to follow Him, you will automatically be drawn into a process of transformation that will steadily change you into God's likeness.

> . . . we all . . . are changed into the same image [of the Lord Jesus] from glory to glory, even as by the Spirit of the Lord.
>
> **2 Corinthians 3:18**

Before you will be able to understand the full benefits as well as the consequences of this verse, you must allow me to share a neglected truth with you. There is a natural as well as a spiritual aspect to the biblical word *glory*, for the biblical term *glory* means much more than the traditional definition implies. This most interesting word goes far beyond merely meaning a lustrous glow that emanates from God and those things He touches. Surprising as it may seem, many times the word *glory* is used in the Bible to describe monetary wealth.

This meaning of the word is unmistakable in scriptures such as: *"Be not thou afraid when one is made rich, when the **glory** of His house is increased; For when he dieth he shall carry nothing away: His **glory** shall not descend after him"* (Psalms 49:16,17). It would be totally out of the biblical context to believe the word glory in this verse is speaking of the lustrous glow of God's favor and anointing, and that at death this divine illumination would not follow the believer into the next life.

This is not the only place the word *glory* is used to describe material wealth. The very first time the Holy Spirit ever uses the word *glory* in Scripture, He uses it to describe monetary wealth and treasure.

> [Jacob] . . . heard the word's of Laban's sons, saying, Jacob hath taken away all that was our father's; and of that which was our father's hath he gotten all this *glory*.
>
> **Genesis 31:1**

In many other portions of Scripture *glory* also refers to monetary wealth.

> **The silver is mine, and the gold is mine, saith the Lord of hosts.**

**The glory of this latter house shall be greater than of the former, saith the Lord of hosts. . . .**

**Haggai 2:8,9**

With this in mind, there can come a much broader understanding when God's Word tells us we are being changed from glory to glory into the marvelous image of Jesus Christ. Beyond the obvious meaning there is a secondary natural meaning, for it is also God's intention that you steadily grow into that part of His glory that pertains to His great material riches. Without the wealth that God has in reserve for you, you will not be able to properly accomplish all of the wonderful projects He has planned for you.

## — SOMETHING IS OBVIOUSLY WRONG —

It is painfully clear that the lack of sufficient funds is prevalent throughout the Church, especially when you realize that most of God's children have been instructed to do grand and marvelous things for Him. However, the agonizing truth is evident, for there almost never seems to be enough money to begin, much less properly finish most of the projects God assigns. Shameful as it may be, the precious children of God, with hearts full of love and compassion, have to spend the greater part of their lives only dreaming about accomplishing their *"unfunded mandates."*

These unfunded or under-funded mandates are evident throughout the length and breadth of the Church. For example, Jesus said to go into the entire world and make disciples of all humanity. I must ask this simple question. After 2,000 years of trying, have we even come close to accomplishing this command? The answer is no! The next question is simple. What has hindered world evangelism more than any other thing? *It has been the lack of money!* Lend an ear and hear just a few of the under-funded mandates that are still incomplete.

- Complete fulfillment of the Great Commission to go into the entire world and make disciples of all creatures (Matthew 28:18-20)

- Appropriation of the absolutely necessary buildings and equipment the Church so desperately needs at this very moment

- Proper funding of orphanages to care for the millions of orphaned and cast away children throughout the world

- Development of sufficient well-stocked food distribution centers to feed the hungry people of this world

The embarrassing truth is that several properly funded soft drink companies have already evangelized the nations of this world, and it didn't take them 2,000 years to get the job done. The soda pop companies have accomplished their evangelistic campaign in less than 100 years. The fact is that secular enterprises that deal in worldwide distribution have only one advantage over the Church. They have more than enough money to fund and sustain their evangelistic outreaches.

## — INCREASE BY SEEDTIME AND HARVEST —

The harsh reality is that the Church has a superior system of financial increase over the secular realm, for secular society has to increase by modest rates. The Church has an optimum system of increase that can range from thirty to sixty to hundredfold. It is a proven system that has brought results to all those who have been informed and put it to work in their finances. Living according to

God's tried and proven system of seedtime and harvest (giving proper offerings and reaping abundant financial harvests), will manifest the finances needed to fund any and every mandate God has ever given. Not only that, but the faithful operation of it will always allow God's children to reflect His true nature to all that see the greater works He accomplishes through them.

We see the power of seedtime and harvest demonstrated in the life of Isaac.

> **Isaac planted crops in that land and the same year reaped a hundredfold, because the Lord blessed him. The man became rich, and his wealth continued to grow until he became very wealthy. He had so many flocks and herds and servants that the Philistines envied him.**
>
> **Genesis 26:12-14 NIV**

Notice the biblical purpose for God prospering Isaac goes far beyond merely publicizing God's goodness to him. It is there to encourage all God's children to participate in the unfailing system of increase that comes through seedtime and harvest. The Book of Hebrews dedicates an entire chapter to preserving for us all the marvelous things God did for the saints of the Old Testament. Isaac is included in this listing of victorious overcomers. However, no matter how greatly God moved in blessing them, we of the New Covenant have God's unfailing promise that He will do even greater things for us.

> **And these men of faith, though they trusted God and won his approval, none of them received all that God had promised them; for God wanted them to wait and share the *even better rewards that were prepared for us.***
>
> **Hebrews 11:39,40 TLB**

It is common knowledge that a promise is only as good as the one who guarantees to fulfill it. The promises of God are sure, for Jesus is the one who makes these better promises, and He is the one who ever lives to bring them to pass.

**Jesus Christ the same yesterday, and to day, and for ever.**

**Hebrews 13:8**

In other words, anything Jesus has done before, He stands ready, willing and able to do again. The Bible also tells us if He did something special for Isaac or anyone else, He is willing to do it for you.

**. . . Peter opened his mouth, and said, Of a truth I perceive that God is no respecter of persons.**

**Acts 10:34**

## — A WORD OF INSTRUCTION —

With all these promises of increase in mind, let me bring some biblical balance. You must never allow the riches of God to become a stumbling block of personal pride. Instead, God's abundant blessings should always be a reason for His children to praise Him for His goodness. Please note that this isn't just idle talk, for the Bible tells us there is a real danger that can come from not staying focused on the purpose of God's blessings to us.

**When you have eaten and are satisfied, praise the Lord your God for the good land he has given you. Be careful that you do not forget the Lord your God, failing to observe his commands, his laws and his decrees that I am giving you this day. Otherwise, when you eat and are satisfied, when you build fine houses and settle down, and when your herds and flocks grow large and your silver and gold increase and all you have is multiplied, then your**

heart will become proud and you will forget the Lord your God, who brought you out of Egypt, out of the land of slavery. He led you through the vast and dreadful desert, that thirsty and water-less land, with its venomous snakes and scorpions. He brought you water out of hard rock. He gave you manna to eat in the desert, something your fathers had never known, to humble and to test you so that in the end it might go well with you. You may say to yourself, "My power and the strength of my hands have produced this wealth for me." *But remember the Lord your God, for it is he who gives you the ability to produce wealth,* and so confirms his covenant, which he swore to your forefathers, as it is today.

**Deuteronomy 8:10-18 NIV**

Every true steward of God must constantly give thought to this warning, for the Bible also says that pride is the forerunner of destruction.

**Pride goeth before destruction, and an haughty spirit before a fall.**

**Proverbs 16:18**

— BE A BLESSING —

Yes, all believers have the power to get wealth. However, God always gives this power for a specific purpose. He gives it to His children so they can be a blessing to all the families of the earth (Genesis 12:1-3). Let this truth take root in your thinking and become a part of your new mindset. *You are empowered by God to get wealth so that you can be a redistributor of his wealth!* Here is a simple question that will help bring even more clarity to the understanding of the truth that God really desires to prosper you. If God did not intend for you to be rich, why would He openly declare that He has given you the power to get wealth?

But remember the Lord your God, for *it is he who gives you the ability to produce wealth,* and so confirms his covenant, which he swore to your forefathers, as it is today.

**Deuteronomy 8:18 NIV**

From the beginning of this book, I have been showing you scripture upon scripture that establishes this truth—Jehovah God wants you to live in abundance. He wants to bless you (empower you to prosper) so that you can be a blessing. If you walk as God wants you to walk, you will live a blessed life, and you will be a blessing.

## — RICH CHILDREN REFLECT THE CHARACTER OF THEIR RICH GOD —

It must become a conscious reality to every believer that our lifestyle graphically illustrates to the world the nature of our God. When unsaved people observe Christians who love the Lord and try to be like Him, they are seeing a part of God's nature. They should notice that these believers live peaceful lives, have comfortable homes and are financially prosperous. They should also see us giving generously to the Church as well as world evangelism and hunger relief. When this happens, those who are observing us will begin to understand that we know something about God that others have overlooked. The good lives we live both spiritually and physically will cause them to realize there must be a force beyond the natural realm moving in our lives. It is a biblical fact that people who walk in harmony with God display by their lives the nature of their God.

Let your light so shine before men, that they may see your good works, and glorify your Father which is in heaven.

**Matthew 5:16**

When believers demonstrate to the world that their God is a rich, generous, caring God, one that has the best interest of His children at heart, untold millions will turn to our God and join in the good life they have seen Him give to His obedient children.

## — SHUN THE LIFESTYLE OF GREED —

God's children should never seek to acquire wealth from the flawed motivation of keeping up with the Joneses. Instead, motivation for gaining wealth should always be that of keeping up with the plan God has for their lives. It is interesting to note that greed almost always stems from the false pride of ownership, while gratitude steadily grows out of the operation of a proper stewardship for God. It is through the process of seedtime and harvest that God graciously gives His children the ability to create an ever-increasing stream of wealth that constantly brings glory to God and His Kingdom. It is obvious from their lifestyles that the truly rich children of the rich God of heaven are not building their own kingdom. Instead, they are involved in an ongoing joint effort with God to build His Kingdom. Their utmost desire and primary motivation will always be to draw all men to the more abundant, everlasting life that Jesus Christ has made available.

## —DEVELOPING A NEW PERCEPTION —

The more you take hold of these principles, the more you will notice a difference in the way you perceive the things God places under your control. You'll see that His abundant supply goes far beyond merely helping you meet your obligations. You will see the ever-expanding potential for increase coming from God to you. When you are operating a true stewardship, people who speak with you will feel as if they are speaking with the personal representative of the rich God of heaven. When this starts to happen, it will be a confirmation to you that the *Apostle Peter was speaking about you when he said, ". . . you are a chosen people. You are a kingdom of priests, God's holy nation, his very own possession. This is so you can show others the goodness of God. . ."* (1 Peter 2:9 NLT).

Only those who are proper stewards of God are His real representatives here on earth. It is interesting to note that when the prodigal son returned to his father's house, his father didn't give him an empty handshake. Instead, he gave him a precious golden ring to wear (Luke 15:22). This signet ring was a mark of identification, for it signified to everyone that he was a son in good standing with a wealthy father. By virtue of this special signet ring, he was authorized to transact business on behalf of his father. When he spoke, it was as if his father were speaking. When others transacted business with him, they knew it was the same as dealing directly with the father. In much the same way, God's stewards represent their Heavenly Father here on earth. He has given us the right to use the name of His Son Jesus by whose power and authority we carry out the royal business of the Kingdom of God.

Every qualified steward always transacts the Father's business in the same way that He would. This is done by allowing the divine nature of your Heavenly Father to operate in and through you. When you conduct the business of your Heavenly Father in this way, you will see an immediate change in your life and your surroundings, for the divine favor of God will quickly cause things to start moving *for you* instead of *against you.*

- You will become the head and not the tail (Deuteronomy 28:13).

- You will begin to experience favor.

- Old enemies will grow powerless; their conflicts with you will diminish and even fade away. *"When a man's ways please the Lord, he maketh even his enemies to be at peace with him"* (Proverbs 16:7).

- The abundant riches of heaven will start to flow to you to enable you to bring about the Father's plans. *". . . no matter what you ask for from the Father, using my name, he will give it to you"* (John 15:16 TLB).

## — THE WALK OF A PROPER STEWARD —

Those who are proper stewards of God walk in an ongoing communion and counsel with God. This allows them to miss the pitfalls of man's flawed wisdom, making it possible for them to experience the ever-increasing wealth that comes from the wise counsel of their God.

> **Oh, the joys of those who do not follow evil men's advice, who do not hang around with sinners, scoffing at the things of God: But they delight in doing everything God wants them to, and day and night are always meditating on his laws and thinking about ways to follow him more closely.**

> **They are like trees along a river bank bearing luscious fruit each season without fail. Their leaves shall never wither, *and all they do shall prosper.***

> **Psalm 1:1-3 TLB**

> **Thus saith the Lord, thy Redeemer, the Holy One of Israel; I am the Lord thy God which teacheth thee to profit, which leadeth thee by the way that thou shouldest go.**

> **Isaiah 48:17**

**. . . those who are led by the Spirit of God are sons of God.**

**For you did not receive a spirit that makes you a slave again to fear, but you received the Spirit of sonship. And by him we cry, "Abba, Father."**

**Romans 8:14,15 NIV**

Proper stewards are not swayed by the opinions of man, nor are they moved by adverse circumstances that rise up against them. They understand that God is sovereign in all He does. Stewards understand that if they are under the control of God, the things He instructs them to do become sovereign directives that cannot be stopped by man or devil.

It takes faith to conduct God's business in a proper manner. Often God shows you the way only one step at a time. Only those who are able to allow God's Spirit to enlighten their spirits will be able to stay faithful to His directives. Proper stewards never work at their stewardship in a half-hearted, uncommitted way. Neither do they shrink from difficult situations. Instead, they are quick to seek the Father's counsel and careful to apply His instructions. This course of action always sees them through to a victorious conclusion.

**. . . thanks be to God, Who in Christ always leads us in triumph [as trophies of Christ's victory] and through us spreads and makes evident the fragrance of the knowledge of God everywhere.**

**2 Corinthians 2:14 Amplified**

## — EMPOWERED TO CREATE WEALTH —

The divine nature that God has put inside of His children makes them unique from any other creature. This new nature is a duplicate of His own nature and brings with it a God-given ability to create wealth (Deuteronomy 8:18).

> **Yours, O LORD, is the greatness and the power and the glory and the majesty and the splendor, for *everything* in heaven and earth is yours. Yours, O LORD, is the kingdom; you are exalted as head over all.**
>
> ***Wealth and honor come from you;* you are the ruler of all things. In your hands are strength and power to exalt and give strength to all.**
>
> ***Now, our God, we give you thanks, and praise your glorious [rich and illustrious] name.***
>
> **1 Chronicles 29:11-13 NIV**

When a believer stops struggling to get wealth and starts seeking a clear understanding of the Father's purpose for wealth, that understanding always brings increase with it. That is exactly how wealth came to King Solomon. Wisdom and understanding came first, and then wealth followed.

> **God said to Solomon, "Since . . . you have not asked for wealth, riches or honor . . . *but for wisdom and knowledge* to govern my people over whom I have made you king, therefore wisdom and knowledge will be given you. And I will also give you *wealth, riches and honor. . . .*"**
>
> **2 Chronicles 1:11,12 NIV**

In that same way, you will be empowered to create wealth when you learn to put your self-serving agendas aside and take up God's sovereign agenda. Remember that it was Jesus who said His followers should deny their own agendas and take up their crosses to follow Him.

> **Then Jesus said to His disciples, If anyone desires to be My disciple, let him deny himself [disregard, lose sight of, and forget**

**himself and his own interests] and take up his cross and follow
Me. . . .**

**Matthew 16:24 Amplified**

Jesus reinforced this truth when He told us that a person
couldn't serve two masters, for he will love one and hate the other.
Giving priority to your own personal agenda will always turn into
a stumbling block that will prevent you from receiving all that
God has for you. It has been said before, but it bears repeating. If
Jesus is to be Lord *at all,* He must be Lord *of all.*

## — GOD'S WAYS ARE NOT MAN'S WAYS —

When Jesus told Peter to go to the lake and cast in a line to
catch a miracle fish, He also told Him to look in the fish's mouth
where he would find some miracle money[1] (Matthew 17:27). It is
common knowledge that Peter was a fisherman. Now please notice
that if Peter were going to experience a miracle increase, he would
not be able to lean to his own understanding. He would have to
exercise complete confidence in our Lord's instructions. As a fisherman, it would be Peter's practical understanding that fish didn't
have coins in their mouths. He had no doubt seen inside thousands of fish's mouths and had never found a coin. Nevertheless,
Peter faithfully obeyed that which was contrary to his natural
understanding. This act of faith in His Lord's instructions brought
him a financial reward. It should be obvious from this example and
others in God's Word that the only profitable course of action for
believers is to allow the mind of Christ to have preeminence over
their own ability to reason and strategize.

**Let this mind be in you, which was also in Christ Jesus.**

**Philippians 2:5**

## — RICH CHILDREN ENJOY HIS RICHES —

As God's rich children, we have been given dominion over the natural realm. This dominion includes the management of this earth and its vast assets.

> **So God created man in his own image, in the image of God created he him; male and female created he them.**
>
> **And God blessed them, and God said unto them, *Be fruitful, and multiply,* and replenish the earth, and subdue it: and *have dominion* over the fish of the sea, and over the fowl of the air, and over every living thing that moveth upon the earth.**
>
> **Genesis 1:27,28**

When Adam and Eve disobeyed God in the Garden of Eden, they unwittingly turned this dominion over to Satan. The fall also abruptly ended mankind's privilege of enjoying the opulent lifestyle of the splendid garden. However, very early in the history of mankind, God started removing the penalties of this curse. His first step was to remove the curse from the ground, thereby allowing the earth to once again flourish in seedtime and harvest. This becomes obvious when you compare Genesis 3:17 with Genesis 8:20,21. The curse came upon the ground through Adam's disobedience.

> **. . . cursed is the ground for thy sake; in sorrow shalt thou eat of it all the days of thy life.**
>
> **Genesis 3:17**

Through Noah's righteous offering, the ground began to prosper once again.

> **And Noah builded an altar unto the Lord; and took of every clean beast, and of every clean fowl, and offered burnt offerings on the altar.**

> **And the Lord smelled a sweet savour; and the Lord said in His heart, *I will not again curse the ground any more for man's sake*. . . .**
>
> **Genesis 8:20,21**

According to the Apostle Paul, we see that with the death and resurrection of our Lord, all remaining semblance of the curse was removed from all those who accept the Lord Jesus Christ as their Savior:

> **Christ hath redeemed us from the curse of the law, being made a curse for us: for it is written, Cursed is every one that hangeth on a tree:**
>
> **That the *blessing* of Abraham might come on the Gentiles through Jesus Christ; that we might receive the promise of the Spirit through faith.**
>
> **Galatians 3:13,14**

As the redeemed children of the Lord, we are once again invited by God to step forward and enjoy the fullness of His glory. However, this time we are invited into the unshakable glory that came into being with the atonement of Jesus Christ. It is of the utmost importance to remember that our Lord's glory is two-dimensional, for it is spiritual as well as natural. While God's Spirit is working on the inner man to bring forth the process of glorious sanctification, He also stands ready to empower the outer man to prosper in material wealth.

Remember there are two ways the word *glory* is used in the Old Testament. In its first usage, the Hebrew word *cabod* describes material wealth (Genesis 31:1). It is also used in this way in many other places. Then it is also used in some places to describe the splendid outer garment of God's glory as well as the manifestation of His divine nature in His children.

For clarification of this truth, let's take another look at just a few more places that the word *glory* describes wealth and natural abundance.

- Genesis 31:1 records that Jacob had taken all of Laban's wealth (*cabod*).

- Psalm 49:17 declares that a man's riches (*cabod*) cannot follow him into the grave.

- Solomon writes that the wise man that follows after righteousness and mercy will find life, righteousness and honor (*cabod*) (Proverbs 21:21).

- Proverbs 22:4 declares, *"By humility and the fear of the Lord are riches, and honor (cabod), and life."*

- Solomon reflects in Ecclesiastes 6:2, *"A man to whom God hath given riches, wealth, and honor (cabod), so that he wanteth nothing for his soul of all that he desireth. . . ."*

The Word of God says He desires to change your inner man by His Spirit from glory to glory. He also desires to put into your hands the glory, or the actual wealth of His infinite riches enabling you to properly function as His well-funded steward. God has not planned for your work in the Kingdom to be drudgery or the menial work of a slave. Rather, He envisions you as a well-funded steward who is *". . . stedfast, unmoveable, always abounding in the work of the Lord, forasmuch as ye know that your labour is not in vain in the Lord"* (1 Corinthians 15:58).

It is nothing more than religious tradition that demands that you wait until you get to heaven to enjoy the riches of God's Kingdom. This unscriptural superstition has been circulating in the Church for centuries. However, Jesus clearly states that you don't have to wait until you get to heaven to enjoy your portion of this world's wealth. He says *". . . [givers] shall receive an hundredfold now is this time. . ."* (Mark 10:30).

God wants you to enjoy everything He has prepared for you, and best of all, you won't have to wait until you get to heaven to enjoy it. You can start today!

## — THE RICHES OF GOD'S GLORY ARE FOR YOU —

Now here is an important truth. The riches of God are not given to you just for establishing His Kingdom. God also desires for you to have more than enough glory (wealth) for you and your loved ones to enjoy the good life. God's plan is for you to have the good life in such abundance that neither you nor your loved ones will want for any good thing that is in the earth.

**"For I know the plans I have for you," declares the Lord, "plans to prosper you and not to harm you, plans to give you hope and a future."**

**Jeremiah 29:11 NIV**

**. . . ye shall come unto . . . a large land: for God hath given it into your hands; a place where *there is no want of any thing that is in the earth.***

**Judges 18:10**

**And you will be called priests of the LORD, you will be named ministers of our God. *You will feed on the wealth of nations,* and in their riches you will boast.**

**Instead of their shame my people will receive a double portion, and instead of disgrace they will rejoice in their inheritance; and *so they will inherit a double portion* in their land, and everlasting joy will be theirs.**

**Isaiah 61:6,7 NIV**

Child of God, keep your faith high and your spiritual eyes wide open, for the manifestation of your glorious inheritance is as sure as the promise of your salvation. Paul writes, *"I pray also that the eyes of your heart may be enlightened in order that you may know the hope to which he has called you, the riches of his glorious inheritance in the saints"* (Ephesians 1:18,19 NIV). God has equipped you with His own nature, His mind and His power, which He wants you to use to their full potential to bring you into all the wealth and prosperity you will ever need.

God's plan is to give you a hope and a bright future. He doesn't have even one day of poverty, failure or sickness planned for you. He loves you too much for that. He created you to be an overcomer, not to be overcome! *"He that overcometh shall inherit all things; and I will be his God, and he shall be my son"* (Revelation 21:7).

One of the biggest roadblocks on the path of God's plan will always be the small-minded, busted and disgusted, broke thinking that the religionists have sowed into the Church. Remember it is God Himself who has made the promise to deliver the wealth of this world into your hands. It is the mighty God of heaven and earth that has predestined you to rule and reign with Him (Revelation 20:6).

Just think of the great benefits that come to all that live in the way that God has planned for them. This means God wants you, as His blood-bought child, to:

- Live in the divine health that Jesus Christ secured for you

- See others healed through the power God releases through you

- Walk with peace in your heart and mind

- Have the victory over every attack the devil dares send your way

- Have a totally new anointing that will move you into the victory each and every time you step out on behalf of God and His Kingdom

- Have more than enough of everything to be blessed and to be a blessing to all the families of the earth

- One day enter into heaven to hear the greatest words any human being could ever hear: "Well done good and faithful steward."

With this mindset, you will be able to boldly say, *"Speak to me God and show me where you want me to sow and how much you want me to give. From this day on, you can count on me to sow big so that you will be released to fund my stewardship in a really big way!"*

---

[1] If you would like to receive a free copy of the book, *Miracle Money,* send your request to John Avanzini Ministries at the address in the back of this book.

*Jesus not only sent His Church
forward with the spiritual authority
to fulfill the Great Commission,
He also provided us with all the
natural resources we would need
to fulfill His command.*

# RICH GOD, RICH CHURCH

## CHAPTER 6

Over the ages of Church history, the traditions of men have institutionalized poverty, deceptively turning it into a spiritual virtue. A brief overview of Church tradition will help you understand how the spirit of poverty entered the Church and how it became an accepted doctrine.

The Roman Catholic Church has considered the practice of taking the vow of poverty as a virtue for centuries. This erroneous belief crossed over to become a tradition in the Protestant churches as well. Based on a flawed interpretation of Matthew 8:20 and Matthew 19:21, the early Catholic fathers and monastic orders often promoted poverty as a virtuous way to obtain right standing with God.

— GOOD INTENTIONS, BAD DOCTRINE —

- *St. Thomas Aquinas:* The classic theologian, St. Thomas Aquinas, properly argued that *"poverty has no intrinsic goodness."* In spite of this, he went on to sing the praises of poverty by saying it *". . . is good only because it is useful to remove the obstacles which stand in the way of the pursuit of spiritual perfection"* (St. Thomas, "Contra Gentiles", III, cxxxiii; Suarez, "Dereligione", tr. VII, l. VIII, c. ii, n. 6; Bucceroni, "Inst. theol. mor.", II, 75, n. 31).

Poverty was considered by the Church to be a particularly virtuous lifestyle, especially for a priest, pastor, or missionary to a foreign field. It is worthy of note that Thomas Aquinas and the saints of his day rooted this belief in a selfish inward view. It was their attempt to show themselves more righteous without giving thought to the effect poverty would have on the future funding of world evangelism. This unscriptural view caused them to lose interest in that part of God's Word that instructs the believer in seedtime and harvest as it pertains to increase in finances. This one-sided, unscriptural view caused God's plan for the prosperity of His children to fall out of the mainline teachings of the Church. This was one of the wrong decisions that has made the prosperity doctrine the neglected truth that it is in the traditional church of our day.

- *The Catholic Church and the vow of poverty:* The Roman Catholic Church laid the foundation for poverty that formed the mindset of traditional understanding that now dominates both Protestant and Catholic thinking. This tradition erroneously taught that voluntary poverty, which is the abandonment of everything except the few things that are essential to basic survival, helped a person to move toward a state of spiritual perfection.

This mindset made a fertile breeding ground for the survival and propagation of poverty inside the Church. It actually loosed *"a spirit of poverty"*—one that is now deceptively cloaked in religious garments and defined as follows:

*"The renunciation which is essential and strictly required as the abandonment of all that is superfluous, not that it is absolutely necessary to give up the ownership of all property, but a man must be contented with what is necessary for his own use. Then only is there a real detachment, which sufficiently mortifies the love of riches, cuts off luxury and vainglory, and frees from the care for worldly goods. Cupidity, vainglory, and excessive solicitude are, according to St. Thomas, the three obstacles, which riches put in the way of acquiring perfection."*
(Summa, II-II, Q. clxxxviii, a. 7)

This unscriptural fixation on perfection, when fully understood, required the renunciation of earthly possessions to be of a permanent character. This can be seen by the perpetual vow of poverty, which is still prevalent among many members of the clergy. He went on to say that the warnings and counsels of Jesus Christ were valuable, even to those who did not vow to a state of perfection. They teach men to moderate their desire for riches *"and accept cheerfully the loss or deprivation of them; and they inculcate [teach by frequent repetition or admonition] that detachment from the things of this world, which our Lord taught when He said, "Everyone of you that doth not renounce all that he possesseth, cannot be my disciple"* (Luke xiv 33). (*The Catholic Encyclopedia*, Volume XII, Copyright © 1911 by Robert Appleton Company Online Edition Copyright © 1999 by Kevin Knight)

I must now allow the Scriptures to speak, for the Word of God clearly states that poverty is a very undesirable condition for any servant of God, especially a preacher of the gospel. The Bible says that people generally do not listen or take instruction from those who are poor.

This wisdom have I seen also under the sun, and it seemed great unto me:

There was a little city, and few men within it; and there came a great king against it, and besieged it, and built great bulwarks against it:

Now there was found in it a poor wise man, and he by his wisdom delivered the city; yet no man remembered that same poor man.

Then said I, Wisdom is better than strength: *nevertheless the poor man's wisdom is despised, and his words are not heard.*

**Ecclesiastes 9:13-16**

It is hard to understand how the theologians and religious leaders of the past, men of God who were supposed to dedicate themselves to the study of God's Word, could have overlooked such a clear contradiction to the poverty doctrine they were formulating. Not only that, but when Jesus spoke of renouncing all that a person possesses, it wasn't a command to enter a state of poverty. Neither was it an invitation to the clergy to take a vow of poverty. When taken in its proper context, it is the first step toward becoming a steward of God. In becoming a proper steward, all ownership of material goods is surrendered, and there is an acknowledgement that everything you control is the property of God. Just a few verses beyond the ninth chapter of Ecclesiastes we find yet another truth in favor of the believer having an abundance of money!

. . . money answereth all things.

**Ecclesiastes 10:19**

- *Honorious III:* Dominican priests also endorsed poverty as a spiritual virtue. Honorious III wrote about these monks in

1217 as, *"filled with the fervor of the Spirit and free from the burden of the possessions of the rich, with firm resolve they [the Dominicans] devoted their life to preaching the Gospel. They went about their duties with great humility and lived a life of voluntary, poverty, exposing themselves to innumerable dangers and sufferings, for the salvation of others."*

Even though these dedicated monks sincerely believed they could please God by forsaking everything of a material nature, this in no way alters the teaching of the Scripture, especially in light of the verse that clearly states that only faith pleases God (Hebrews 11:6). Get a firm hold on this truth. *God is not impressed by what we are willing to do without in an attempt to please Him.* Instead, the Word of God tells us God is highly impressed with the proper operation of a person's assigned stewardship. Matthew 25 tells us He rewards those who increase and greatly multiply the material goods He entrusts into their hands.

**After a long time the lord of those servants cometh, and reckoneth with them.**

**And so he that had received five talents came and brought other five talents, saying, Lord, thou deliveredst unto me five talents: behold, I have gained beside them five talents more.**

**His lord said unto him, Well done, thou good and faithful servant: thou hast been faithful over a few things, I will make thee ruler over many things: enter thou into the joy of thy lord.**

**Matthew 25:19-21**

Now don't miss this great truth. Reward for proper behavior does not come to the steward because he abandons the wealth his lord gave him. Quite the opposite is true, for in this parable, one of the stewards does detach himself from the wealth his lord entrusted to him. The parable goes on to tell us the poverty-minded steward was severely reprimanded and separated from his master.

> . . . I was afraid, and went, and hid thy talent in the earth: lo, there thou hast that is thine.

> His lord answered and said unto him, Thou wicked and slothful servant, thou knewest that I reap where I sowed not, and gather where I have not strawed [scattered seed]:

> Thou oughtest therefore to have put my money to the exchangers, and then at my coming I should have received mine own with usury.

> Take therefore the talent from him. . . .

> And cast ye the unprofitable servant into outer darkness: there shall be weeping and gnashing of teeth.

> Matthew 25:25-28,30

- *Franciscans and Dominicans:* Following the examples of St. Francis of Assisi and St. Dominic, many monastic orders and religious groups blindly followed suit and adopted poverty as a virtuous lifestyle.

To this day the mistaken notion that the tradition of poverty somehow represents spiritual virtue is still propagated by many churches. Even as you are reading this book, pastors, missionaries and full time Christian workers, totally without any scriptural instructions to do so, are bowing before denominational altars and taking vows of poverty. The heartbreak of this is twofold, for it will deprive them as well as the masses of people who hear them from having all that God has in store for them. The false doctrine of poverty propagates by bringing forth more and more religious leaders that will make the same mistake of taking the vow of poverty as well as passing it on to future generations.

Let me now draw your attention to the fact that the doctrine of poverty is not a purely Catholic doctrine, for many of the great ministers of the Protestant Church have embraced and even glorified it.

- *Martin Luther and John Calvin:* Their traditional roots were founded in poverty. Before the Reformation, Martin Luther was an Augustinian monk who was required to live a life of poverty under the strictest of monastic rules. His life consisted of dedicated study of the Scriptures as well as an ongoing practice of sacrificing all material possessions. With the reformation, Luther left the monastic lifestyle. However, much of the poverty mindset of his earlier religious training remained firmly entrenched in his thinking. In that same way, John Calvin began his reforming work with the religious mindset of his early training in the poverty doctrine.

The influence of the root of poverty that Satan so skillfully planted in the Church is obvious in the writings of many of God's great servants. It is a paradox that those who could bless us so greatly with the revelations that are synonymous with their names would unwittingly propagate from generation to generation the poisonous doctrine of poverty. Little did they realize their erroneous embracing of poverty was bringing the Church to the most expensive time in the history of mankind with empty pockets and no scriptural insight or information about God's plan for divine increase.

- *Charles Spurgeon:* As surprising as it may seem, it was Charles Spurgeon, one of the great pastors of the 19th century that made the following declaration: *Oh! may God send us poverty; may God send us lack of means,* and take away our power of speech if it must be, and help us only to stammer, if we may only thus get the blessing. Oh! I crave to be useful to souls, and all the rest may go where it will. And each church must crave the same. "Not by might, nor by power, but by my Spirit, saith the Lord." Instead of despising the day of small things, we ought to be encouraged. It is by the small things that God seems to work, but the great things he does not often use. He won't have Gideon's great host—let them go to their homes—let the mass of them go. Bring them down to the water: pick out only the men that lap, and then there is a very few. . . . *Never mind your feebleness, brethren, your fewness, your poverty, your want of ability. Throw your souls into God's cause, pray mightily, lay hold on the gates of heaven, stir heaven and earth,* rather than be defeated in winning souls, and you will see results that will astonish you yet. "Who hath despised the day of small things?" (Published on Thursday, December 9th, 1915. Delivered by C. H. Spurgeon, At the Metropolitan Tabernacle, Newington On Lord's-day Evening, 27th, August 1871.)

Let there be no mistake about it. God most certainly uses small things. However, this in no way changes His desire to do things in a big way. God does not have to deprive us of the good things of life in order to use us in His great harvest of souls. In fact, it was God's Word to Abraham that promised abundance so great that Abraham could be a blessing to all the families of the earth (Genesis 12:1-3).

- *Jonathan Edwards:* In his sermon, "The Excellency of Christ," Jonathan Edwards (1703-1758), the great preacher of the first Great Awakening preached that Jesus chose to live in poverty. *". . . contentedly living in the family of Joseph the carpenter, and Mary his mother, for thirty years together, and afterwards choosing outward meanness, poverty, and contempt, rather than earthly greatness; in his washing his disciples' feet, and in all his speeches and deportment towards them."*

Blinded by the erroneous interpretation of the gospels as it pertained to earthly possessions, Jonathan Edwards failed to see the financial assets of Abraham, Isaac, Jacob and Joseph, as well as Jesus Himself. With the financial assets of so many Bible characters clearly proclaimed throughout the Scripture, his eyes remained closed to God's promise to prosper.

We can clearly see the effects of traditional interpretations through the writings of these past great men, for in the matter of God's plan to prosper His Church, it is exactly as Jesus said.

**Making the word of God of none effect through your tradition. . . .**

**Mark 7:13**

- *Charles Finney:* Another Great Awakening revivalist, Charles Finney in the mid-1900s, remarked, *"dwell much upon your temporal and spiritual good things, and spend much time in blessing and thanking God for existence, life, health, sickness, **poverty**, or wealth or whatever his providence has allotted you—that you were born in this age—in this land—under such circumstances. . ."* ("Carefulness a Sin").

In spite of the mistaken views from the past, those of us who are now alive in Christ Jesus must start thanking God for delivering us from the curse of sickness and poverty. We must recognize that neither poverty nor sickness is God's perfect will for His children. *"Beloved, I wish [pray] above all things that thou mayest prosper and be in health, even as thy soul prospereth"* (3 John 2).

In using the preceding comments by these great men from the past, I am not speaking against them nor trying to bring any shame upon them. Many of them were mightily used of God and did much to further the gospel. They deserve our respect and our thanks. These quotations are simply examples of how famous Christian leaders (both Catholic and Protestant) have the ability to release, preserve and propagate an unscriptural doctrine in the Church.

— TRADITION MAKES THE WORD OF GOD OF NO EFFECT —

The Church must become diligent about feeding the saints with the true bread of life (the unadulterated Word of God). By doing so, there will come a rapid deprogramming of the subconscious mindset of poverty that has attached itself to the Body of Christ. Let a word of warning from God's Word go forth to all those who would propagate erroneous traditions. This warning also goes forth from God's Word to those who unquestioningly believe erroneous teachings.

> **"You have let go of the commands of God and are holding on to the traditions of men.**
>
> **"Thus you nullify the word of God by your tradition that you have handed down. . . ."**
>
> **Mark 7:8,13 NIV**

Notice that the biblical context of this warning points directly to traditional *interpretations* of God's Word. It does not speak of the ceremonial traditions, as many would have you believe. It is not the burning of incense or the wearing of clerical robes that makes the Word of God ineffective.

The context is clear; Jesus was talking about the oral traditions of the religious rulers when He said their traditions had made the Word of God of no effect. The written Word was clear in commanding the religious leaders of our Lord's day to honor their elderly parents. However, the oral traditions they honored and respected more than the Word of God permitted them to dedicate their money to the Temple. By this act they placed their money off limits to their elderly parents. Jesus rebuked this unscriptural practice along with the many other religious traditions that kept people from properly fulfilling God's will for their lives.

> **"You have let go of the commands of God and are holding on to the traditions of men."**
>
> **And he said to them: "You have a fine way of setting aside the commands of God in order to observe your own traditions! For Moses said, 'Honor your father and your mother,' and, 'Anyone who curses his father or mother must be put to death.' But you say that if a man says to his father or mother: 'Whatever help you might otherwise have received from me is Corban' (that is, a gift devoted to God), then you no longer let him do anything for his father or mother. Thus you nullify the word of God by your tradition that you have handed down. And you do many things like that."**
>
> **Mark 7:8-13 NIV**

It is amazing how much of God's Word has acquired traditional interpretations that have nothing to do with God's intended meaning. As always, these misinterpreted scriptures play right into Satan's hand, assisting him in keeping the Church poor and powerless. Because of this, the Church's unfounded tradition of poverty persists even to this day. Unknown to those who protect and propagate the doctrine of poverty, these well-meaning but not so well informed leaders assist in prolonging Satan's days in the earth. The devil has unrelentingly used the manmade traditions of poverty to maintain a mindset among God's people that it is more spiritual to be poor than rich. This mindset has stood in the way of every revival and mission outreach since it was first spawned into the Church. However, when the Church as a whole returns to the biblical mindset of seedtime and harvest, everything the Church so desperately needs to properly carry out our Lord's directions will quickly fall into our hands.

The only hope for this to happen is for the Church to adopt the "Berean mindset." The Bereans never took tradition or the word of man as truth until they had diligently searched the Scriptures to see if that which they were being taught was found in the Word of God. The Bereans *". . . were more noble than those in Thessalonica, in that they received the word with all readiness of mind, and searched the scriptures daily, whether those things were so"* (Acts 17:11).

## — THE EASY-ISM OF OUR DAY —

One of the great disgraces of the modern-day Church is that its members find it easier to accept without question what their favorite religious leaders say instead of diligently searching the Scripture for themselves to verify that the things they are being taught are true. Do not let the thought of searching the Scripture frighten you, for Jesus promises that the Holy Spirit will guide you into all truth.

**Howbeit when he, the Spirit of truth, is come, *he will guide you into all truth:* for he shall not speak of himself; but whatso-**

**ever he shall hear, that shall he speak: and he will shew you things to come.**

**John 16:13**

When it comes to properly living the life of a believer, it matters little what man has to say. What really matters is what God's Word has to say!

The Apostle Paul gave a stern warning to those who do not apply themselves to growing up in Christ.

> **If you belong to Christ, then you are Abraham's seed, and heirs according to the promise.**
>
> **What I am saying is that** *as long as the heir is a child, he is no different from a slave, although he owns the whole estate.*

**Galatians 3:29; 4:1**

Here we see that as long as believers remain childish in their understanding, their childishness puts all of their rightful inheritance beyond their reach. You may be one of those who by your birthright owns the whole estate. Yet you may have absolutely nothing to show for it, all because of a childish understanding. As long as the mindset of the baby Christian prevails, God's best for you will not be allowed to manifest.

Like a hired servant, the immature believer does not qualify for the privileges that accompany full stewardship. Looking again at the example of the three stewards of Matthew 25, we see this truth. The steward who received the one talent dealt with it in an immature manner. He foolishly buried it. It is obvious the master expected him to increase that which was entrusted to him, for we see that when the first two stewards began to walk in maturity, the good master released more and more wealth into their hands.

Mature sons and daughters learn from their father as well as their own experience how to properly manage that which has been committed to them.

Every believer is a child of God, but not every child of God is a mature believer. Moving into maturity is one of the primary expectations the Father has of His children. To help fulfill this expectation, God provides the five-fold ministry to help His sons and daughters grow up in Him.

> . . . he gave some, apostles; and some, prophets; and some, evangelists; and some, pastors and teachers;
>
> For the perfecting of the saints, for the work of the ministry, for the edifying of the body of Christ:
>
> Till we all come in the unity of the faith, and of the knowledge of the Son of God, unto a perfect man, unto the measure of the stature of the fulness of Christ:
>
> That we henceforth be no more children, tossed to and fro, and carried about with every wind of doctrine, by the sleight of men, and cunning craftiness, whereby they lie in wait to deceive;
>
> But speaking the truth in love, may grow up into him in all things, which is the head, even Christ.
>
> **Ephesians 4:11-15**

— THE TRUE RICHES OF THE CHURCH —

Jesus never intended for His bride, the Church, to be impoverished or suffer any lack. The Bible confirms throughout the Old and New Testaments that the rich God of heaven intended for His Church to have all that they would need to fulfill His Great Commission. In that commission, Jesus not only sent His Church forward with the spiritual authority to fulfill His command, He also promised to provide His bride with all the natural resources she would need to fulfill His wishes. When our Lord said *". . . All power is given unto me in heaven and earth"* (Matthew 28:18), the Greek word He used for power is *exousa,* which means *"privilege, force and capacity."*

**And Jesus came and spake unto them, saying, All power is given unto me in heaven and in earth.**

***Go ye therefore,*** **and teach all nations, baptizing them in the name of the Father, and of the Son, and of the Holy Ghost:**

**Teaching them to observe all things whatsoever I have commanded you: and, lo, I am with you always, even unto the end of the world. Amen.**

**Matthew 28:18-20**

In these marching orders for the Church, Jesus instructs us to go because we have been given all the authority and capacity to accomplish all that He has commanded. Notice that Jesus not only sends us, He also promises to go with us every step of the way! *". . . Go ye therefore . . . and, lo, I am with you always. . ."* (Matthew 28:19,20).

Even earlier in our Lord's ministry, He promised abundant supply of all the natural substance we would need to accomplish His directives.

**. . . Whatsoever ye shall ask the Father in my name, he will give it you.**

**John 16:23**

The Apostle Peter further validated this promise of divine supply by specifying the two realms in which the believer would be supplied.

> **. . . his divine power hath given unto us all things that pertain unto life and Godliness, through the knowledge of him that hath called us to glory and virtue.**
>
> **2 Peter 1:3**

Yes, you are reading correctly. The promise of God covers the physical as well as the spiritual realm.

## — THE GOOD BRIDEGROOM —

It would most surely be abusive for a husband to neglect taking care of his wife. Not clothing, feeding, and nurturing her would reflect badly on him. How much more offensive would it be if Jesus refused to take care of His bride? Leaving the Church floundering in insufficiency would project to the lost of this world that our God is abusive instead of loving, a taker instead of a giver, poor instead of rich. However, we know from the Word of God that our Lord sits on the right hand of our Father in heaven, ever ready to lavish riches and treasure upon His blood-bought Church.

The Song of Solomon portrays Solomon as a type of Jesus Christ, and Solomon's bride as a type of the local church. Listen as Solomon's bride boldly proclaims Solomon's care for her well being.

> **He has taken me to the banquet hall, and his banner over me is love.**
>
> **Song of Solomon 2:4 NIV**

In that same way, Jesus desires to provide a lavish banquet for His bride, a feast that includes all that His bride could ever need or desire.

> **. . . his divine power hath given unto us *all things* that pertain unto *life* and *godliness*. . . .**
>
> **2 Peter 1:3**

To better understand the procedure that was followed in preparing a bride in early eastern culture, it will be helpful if we read a passage from the Book of Esther. In it we see the lavish way in which the bride is made ready for the king she is soon to marry.

> **Each young woman's turn came to go in to King Ahasuerus after she had completed *twelve months' preparation*, according to the regulations for the women, for thus were the days of their preparation apportioned: six months with oil of myrrh, and *six months with perfumes and preparations for beautifying women*.**
>
> **Thus prepared, each young woman went to the king, and *she was given whatever she desired* to take with her from the women's quarters to the king's palace.**
>
> **Esther 2:12,13 NKJV**

In this glimpse of the great supply of expensive oils and perfumes that were unsparingly poured out on those who would be considered for the position of the royal bride, we can be assured that King Jesus would do no less. How could anyone even begin to imagine that a heathen king like Ahasuerus could treat his bride better than the righteous King of Heaven, Jesus Christ?

Notice that the king provided everything necessary to prepare the future queen. No expense was spared, because he wanted the very best for his bride-to-be. There can be no doubt that the King of Heaven would provide even better conditions for His bride. Therefore, we know that King Jesus Christ, our wonderful bridegroom, graciously supplies all that we need or desire to become everything He has called us to be.

It is also interesting to note at this time that the Apostle Paul tells us the Bride of Christ does not primarily come from among the rich and famous of this world.

. . . consider your own call, brethren; not many [of you were considered to be] wise according to human estimates and standards, not many influential and powerful, not many of high and noble birth.

[No] for God selected (deliberately chose) what in the world is foolish to put the wise to shame, and what the world calls weak to put the strong to shame.

And God also selected (deliberately chose) what in the world is low-born and insignificant and branded and treated with contempt, even the things that are nothing, that He might depose and bring to nothing the things that are.

**1 Corinthians 1:26-28 Amplified**

In many cases, the redeemed from among men have little if any wealth of their own when they first come to the Lord. Therefore, it is obvious that if this less than prosperous group called "the Bride of Christ" were going to be lavishly prepared, it would be up to God to foot the bill. Here's the good news; the Word of God says He will freely supply.

He that spared not his own Son, but delivered him up for us all, how shall he not with him also *freely give us all things?*

**Romans 8:32**

Thank God, for the Bride of Christ has a rich bridegroom who freely gives to us everything we need to properly build His Kingdom. In every moral government, it is a part of the marriage agreement that whatever belongs to the groom becomes the joint property of the bride.

The Spirit itself beareth witness with our spirit, that we are the children of God:

**And if children, then heirs; heirs of God, and joint-heirs with Christ. . . .**

**Romans 8:16,17**

In the righteous and moral government of God, the Church has a well-documented claim of joint ownership to all the riches of God's universe. Not only that, but we also have written authority to freely draw on His infinite riches for doing the work of the Kingdom.

**. . . my God shall supply all your need [requirements, requisitions, demands] according to his riches in glory by Christ Jesus.**

**Philippians 4:19**

Anything that keeps the Church poor is in total opposition to the written will of God. Religious errors that teach, or even intimate that God desires His Church to do without are nothing more than unfounded speculation on the part of religious leaders. These are blind guides that have misinterpreted the Word of God, thereby rendering it of no effect in this time when abundance is most needed.

**. . . if the blind lead the blind, both shall fall into the ditch.**

**Matthew 15:14**

## — YOU HAVE A DIVINE MISSION —

If you have read this far, you are probably one of the end-time saints that God has chosen to break the Church loose from the deceptive traditions of insufficiency that have attached themselves to it. My prayer is that you will be the kind of person who will boldly accept the teachings presented from God's Word. Take courage, for the Bible promises that your boldness in this matter will be greatly rewarded. I draw your attention once again to the three stewards of Matthew 25. Two of them moved into their master's direct will by multiplying the investment he had made in them. The third rendered his lord's investment ineffective by his vow of poverty, separating himself from that which God had provided. Our Lord boldly states that the aggressive actions of the first two stewards in producing an increase were rewarded while the fear of the third cost him everything.

> **. . . cast ye the unprofitable servant into outer darkness. . . .**
>
> **Matthew 25:30**

God is calling you to take your place with the wise servants of His Kingdom—those who boldly proclaim His Word about their God's goodness. If you will allow the Spirit of God to operate in your heart as it pertains to God's abundant supply for you and through you, you will see an immediate change begin to take place in and around you. Instead of seeing yourself surrounded with pending disaster, you will see opportunity opening up to you on every side. Your every day problems will change into challenges that crumble before divinely directed victories. If you fall, you will see God immediately lifting you up, wiping clean the slate, and encouraging you to make a fresh start.

Living as a child of the rich God will change your view of life forever. As the blessed offspring of the rich God of heaven, you will find that opportunities await you at every turn in the road. Join me in this prayer.

*"Dear Lord Jesus, you are the Head of the Church. You hold every-thing together; everything belongs to you. I come to you with your blood-bought children. I ask you to activate their covenant promise of abundance and loose to them their rich inheritance. I rebuke the*

*ancient lie of the enemy that keeps your children floundering in insuf-*
*ficiency. I declare that our Bridegroom, Christ Jesus, will adequately*
*provide for us in such a splendid way that nothing we will ever need*
*will be withheld from us. I pray that each of your redeemed children*
*will come to a full realization of the unlimited access they have to*
*everything they need or desire for fulfilling their part in building your*
*great Kingdom. Thank you that all you have promised will come to*
*pass in Christ Jesus. Amen.*

*Faithful stewards always give their
rich Father in heaven praise
for every good and perfect gift
He bestows on them.*

# TAKING PLEASURE IN OUR RICH GOD

## CHAPTER 7

Your relationship with the rich Father of heaven should be one of praise, fellowship, and a joint venture in great accomplishments. It will not be one of constant demands for your finances to support the Father's enterprises and outreaches. Neither will it be a constant struggle on your part to barely get by. You can have this wonderful relationship by listening closely to Him as He gives you direction. To be sure you are hearing from Him, make your times of conversation with God more like this:

- Father, how can I become a better steward so that you can entrust even more responsibility to me? In other words, show me what you want changed in my life, and I will gladly change it.

- Father, guide me so that I can wisely expand the assets you have entrusted to me. In other words, Father, tell me the good-ground ministries into which you want me to sow financial seed.

- Father, be specific with me as to how much I should give each time you instruct me to sow.

- Father, please keep me informed about all the new things you are doing and the part you would have me play in fulfilling them.

- Father, I ask you to bless the seed I am sowing so much that I will have even more financial seed to sow in the future.

- Father, please show me a good place to sow a special seed, even this day.

## — RELEASING GOD'S ASSETS —

A pastor friend of mine in Indonesia has learned how to properly release the assets God has placed under his control. God looked upon his obedience with such favor that his church was able to quickly come out of the bondage of debt making it totally debt-free. He told me the story of how his church had fallen six months behind on their mortgage payments. In desperation, the pastor cried out to God, asking Him to deliver his church from its financial crisis. His first approach was like a spoiled child, begging his Heavenly Father to fix the problem. His cry was, *"Dear God please save me and my church from this debt."*

After a while of having no result from this desperate prayer, he became silent and began to simply listen for God's instructions. Almost as quickly as he stopped his childish begging, God began to speak. His words were straightforward, *"Are you willing to release some of that which I have entrusted to you? Are you willing to sow your new car into the work of the ministry?"* The pastor had just received his first, brand-new car, and best of all, it was totally paid for. Notice the importance of this moment, for almost as quickly as the new automobile had come to him, God was requiring it as a seed. It is important to understand that really successful stewards are always willing to release anything they have at God's command. They know they are not the owners of the assets they control; they are only God's stewards over them.

Even though my pastor friend did not immediately understand all that God was doing, soon he realized that a highly spiritual process was taking place. God was giving him an opportunity to vastly improve the quality of his stewardship. By simply obeying the Lord's command, this pastor would be able to take a spiritual step forward. I am glad to say that he obeyed God and graduated into a much greater level of stewardship than he had previously operated.

As my pastor friend sowed his car as a seed to bring his church out of debt, his example of obedience so inspired his wife that she sowed all of her jewelry into the gospel. The end result of this powerful act of obedience was bigger than anyone could have imagined, for in the next ten months, this Indonesian church was able to pay the church mortgage in full, making them totally debt free.

When I asked the pastor what he had learned from this experience, his answer was so profound that I don't think I will ever forget it. He said, *"Since experiencing that miracle increase, whenever I receive any gift from God, I **immediately** praise Him for it, then I ask this simple question. "Father, have you entrusted this new asset to me for sowing, or is it for me to use for a season?"* By the way, the last time I visited this pastor, he drove me around the city in a brand new debt-free automobile, a much nicer one than he originally sowed. I was also present when his wife was given a beautiful watch that was worth many thousands of dollars. Best of all, they know their increased blessings are a part of their harvest from obediently sowing that which God had instructed.

Take a moment and inventory your goods. Do you have some seed in your barn that is just lying there, inactive and unproductive? Too often, we don't ask God the question this dear pastor asked. *"Lord, how do you want me to use this wonderful gift you have just given me?"* God has a perfect plan for all that He gives you. By simply asking Him what that perfect plan is, you will be assured of finding His perfect will for your stewardship.

It is an established fact that the manner in which we use the resources God gives us determines whether they become a blessing or a curse. For example, you could use lumber to build a home or a gambling hall. In that same way, you have the power to use your assets as an instrument of blessing or cursing. This may sound like a harsh statement. However, some people do use the wealth of this world improperly. Even the money from savings accounts owned by dedicated Christians can be loaned out by their banking institution to enterprises that will bring a curse instead of a blessing to their communities.

Please do not misunderstand, for I am not saying we shouldn't set some money aside. God most certainly wants His children to have savings accounts as well as retirement accounts.

**Blessed shall be thy basket and thy store.**

**Deuteronomy 28:5**

I am saying the real steward never counts any part of the assets he controls to be off limits to God and the advancement of His Kingdom. It is good for the steward of God to periodically take a portion of his funds and sow it into the gospel outreach of the Kingdom. However, as always, those funds must be sown only according to God's direction.

— BLESSED TO BE A BLESSING —

God has plainly stated that it is His plan for you to be a blessing to everyone around you (Genesis 12:1-3). As you tap into

God's infinite supply of wealth, you will be enabled to flow it from your hands into the hands of individuals as well as good-ground ministries. I want you to start thinking of your stewardship in a bold new way. I want you to picture yourself at the foot of Niagara Falls getting a drink of cool, refreshing water. No matter how thirsty you may be or how hard you might try, you will not be able to open your mouth wide enough to catch all the water that is coming your way. In that same way, you can have so much wealth coming to you that you will have an inexhaustible flow of blessing to distribute to others. At the same time, you will have more than enough for your own needs and desires.

> **. . . he that watereth shall be watered also himself.**
>
> **Proverbs 11:25**

Let this picture of a Niagara-sized blessing that constantly flows to you from God become permanently etched on your mind. Try it and you will see that it will bring you the added blessing of peace of mind. That's much better than always worrying about a potential shortage and the possibility of future problems.

## — GIVE THE FATHER PRAISE —

Faithful stewards always give their rich Father in heaven praise for every good and perfect gift He bestows on them. The real steward of God avoids being like the prodigal son (Luke 15) that demanded to receive his father's riches to use as he wanted. Instead, a true steward uses as a role model the faithful stewards of Matthew 25. Those stewards received that which the master had for them and demonstrated their faithfulness by managing their father's wealth in a way that was well pleasing to him.

The fully approved steward of God never allows the deceptive thoughts of personal ownership to take root in his mind. He stands ever ready to cast down any and all evil imaginations of this sort.

> **Casting down imaginations, and every high thing that exalteth itself against the knowledge of God, and bringing into captivity every thought to the obedience of Christ.**
>
> **2 Corinthians 10:5**

Regardless of how an asset comes into the hand of a steward, he is always diligent to keep a clear view of the true source of every asset he controls.

> **But whatever is good and perfect comes to us from God, the Creator of all light, and he shines forever without change or shadow.**
>
> **James 1:17 TLB**

Because of this, your first response to every good gift that comes to you should always be to give thanks to your Father in heaven for the trust He has demonstrated in you by placing it into your care. The next thing you should do is automatically ask God this question. *"Lord, have you released this new asset to me for sowing, or is it for me and my loved ones to use for a season?"*

The Book of Psalms is a rich source of gracious words for praising and thanking God for His goodness to us. Learn to generously use these and other verses like them in praising your rich Father for His goodness to you.

> **I will praise you, O LORD, with all my heart; I will tell of all your wonders.**
>
> **I will be glad and rejoice in you; I will sing praise to your name, O Most High.**
>
> **Psalms 9:1,2 NIV**

From you comes the theme of my praise in the great assembly; before those who fear you will I fulfill my vows.

The poor will eat and be satisfied; they who seek the LORD will praise him—may your hearts live forever!

**Psalms 22:25,26 NIV**

He put a new song in my mouth, a hymn of praise to our God. Many will see and fear and put their trust in the LORD.

Blessed is the man who makes the LORD his trust, who does not look to the proud, to those who turn aside to false gods.

Many, O LORD my God, are the wonders you have done. The things you planned for us no one can recount to you; were I to speak and tell of them, they would be too many to declare.

**Psalms 40:3-5 NIV**

Good stewards praise God every day for all that He has placed under their care. When our focus is on God and His will for our lives, we will give Him praise and thanks for every blessing that we receive, no matter how large or small it may be. In that same way, we will lovingly care for each new asset and use it in accordance with the Master's instructions.

Asking our Heavenly Father to reveal His plan for each asset and faithfully following the principle of thanksgiving will always keep our motivation in line with God's purposes for our lives. When love and gratitude motivate us, no task will be too small or too insignificant to warrant anything less than our most careful attention.

## — LOVE IS A GIFT FROM GOD —

Always remember God gave the first gift ever given, for He gave us His love. There is no way to express love more thoroughly than the way God showed it to mankind.

> **For God so loved the world, that he gave his only begotten Son, that whosoever believeth in him should not perish, but have everlasting life.**

> **For God sent not his Son into the world to condemn the world; but that the world through him might be saved.**

> **John 3:16,17**

Try as we may, we can never out love or out give our rich God. Not only do we have the promise of eternal life through the matchless gift of God's love, but we also have a solemn promise that our new birth will bring an abundant life (John 10:10). This abundance is always ready to overflow from the storehouses of our rich and loving God. In fact, we have the right to participate in the very same promises that God gave to Abraham. *"And now that you belong to Christ, you are the true children of Abraham. You are his heirs, and now all the promises God gave to him belong to you"* (Galatians 3:29 NLT). Add to this the expanded explanation that Simon Peter gives of the all-inclusive promises that come to us with our salvation.

> **According as his divine power *hath given unto us all things that pertain unto life and Godliness,* through the knowledge of him that hath called us to glory and virtue:**

> **Whereby are given unto us exceeding great and precious promises: that by these ye might be partakers of the divine nature. . . .**

> **2 Peter 1:3,4**

With the specific details that Simon Peter gives, we can see that not only do God's promises overflow with spiritual blessings, they also include an abundance of all the many things that pertain to the natural realm of life.

Notice that these verses state that God has already fulfilled every need and met every desire we could ever experience. The more you understand this truth, the more confidence it will build within you. Thank God that He designed our daily lives in Christ to be so much more than distasteful obligations, tedious duties, and traditional acts of religious worship. God wants you, as His obedient child and faithful steward, to have exceeding great joy and abundant supply as you serve Him.

> **He that spared not his own Son, but delivered him up for us all, how shall he not with him also freely give us all things?**
>
> **Romans 8:32**

When you consider the promise of eternal life and all that it implies, the answer will forever settle the question as to whether or not God really wants to bless you here on earth. In fact, the more you know about God's goodness, the less you will worry about the things of this world. The Bible says that He will withhold nothing that you desire. There is no limit to how much you can receive, for He has already given you the best there is—His own Son, the Lord Jesus Christ!

## — PROSPERING IN THE ABUNDANCE OF A RICH GOD —

*"He that hath an ear to hear let him hear"* (Mark 4:9). As a faithful steward of God, you can experience ever-increasing prosperity, making it possible for you to generously fund every good work of His Kingdom. The surplus that will come forth from a properly operated stewardship will make it easy for you to demonstrate to the world how good your rich Father really is.

**Let your light so shine before men, that they may see your
good works, and glorify your Father which is in heaven.**

**Matthew 5:16**

Also note that your rich Father wants your stewardship to be
free from the sorrow and misery that comes to those who gain
their wealth by the methods of this present world's system. This
becomes clear when you compare the following two scriptures.

**But they that will be rich fall into temptation and a snare, and
into many foolish and hurtful lusts, which drown men in destruction and perdition.**

**For the love of money is the root of all evil: which while some
coveted after, they have erred from the faith, and *pierced themselves through with many sorrows*.**

**1Timothy 6:9,10**

**The blessing of the LORD makes one rich, And He adds no
sorrow with it.**

**Proverbs 10:22 NKJV**

As always, the purpose of every blessing that comes from God
is to bring joy to the believer. It brings the joy that comes from
obedience; it also brings the joy that comes from funding the end-
time harvest, and it brings the joy that comes from living the good
life to its fullest.

- **Stewards must be faithful with all that God has put into
  their hands.**
  *"Moreover it is **required** in stewards, that a man be found
  faithful"* (1 Corinthians 4:2). The primary requirement for a
  steward is to be faithful in the transaction of the master's
  business. As a steward of God, your business will always be

— 176 —

Kingdom business, whether it is the Kingdom business of your family, the Kingdom business of your secular vocation, or the Kingdom business of God's chosen ministries and enterprises.

- **Stewards must be faithful in tithing.**
Tithing simply returns to the Lord that which already belongs to Him.

> . . . all the tithe of the land, whether of the seed of the land, or of the fruit of the tree, is the Lord's: it is holy unto the Lord.
>
> **Leviticus 27:30**

By tithing, stewards demonstrate four things:

1. They are obedient in financial matters.

2. The wealth they receive is not their own, for it comes from the Master of their stewardship.

3. Heaven will remain open so that their Master will be able to prosper all they do.

4. Faithfulness in tithing also stops the devourer from diminishing the harvest of their stewardship.

> Bring ye all the tithes into the storehouse, that there may be meat in mine house, and prove me now herewith, saith the LORD of hosts, if I will not open you the windows of heaven, and pour you out a blessing, that there shall not be room enough to receive it.
>
> And I will rebuke the devourer for your sakes, and he shall not destroy the fruits of your ground; neither shall your vine cast her fruit before the time in the field, saith the LORD of host.
>
> **Malachi 3:10,11**

- **Stewards must be faithful to sow.**

  Biblical stewards are convinced that the system of increase their Master honors and rewards is seedtime and harvest. Therefore, they are faithful to sow.

  > **Be not deceived; God is not mocked: for whatsoever a man soweth, that shall he also reap.**
  >
  > **Galatians 6:7**

  The mindset of a true steward will not be that of the taker, for his new God-given nature controls him, causing him to be a giver.

- **Stewards who faithfully sow into the Kingdom of God reap in direct proportion to the amount they sow.**

  > **. . . a farmer who plants just a few seeds will get only a small crop, but if *he plants much, he will reap much.***
  >
  > **2 Corinthians 9:6 TLB**

Think about it for a moment. How do you rate yourself as a steward? Are you a willing steward, one who is excited about returning a generous portion of all that God releases to you? All truly faithful stewards realize that God stands ready, willing, and able to make an ever-increasing investment into their stewardship. His investment will be in direct proportion to their willingness to make an ever-increasing investment into His Kingdom.

These Kingdom principles will always be of the utmost importance to every real steward of the rich God of heaven. Too often believers are talked into giving in accordance with a fundraising program or a highly charismatic personality who may be taking an offering. This kind of motivation in giving seldom brings the increase God promises. Proper stewards always remember that it is plentiful seed planted in good soil that brings an abundant harvest. Faithfully sowing financial seed into the ministry as God instructs you is exactly the same as sowing your finances directly into God's own hand.

## — FOUR STEPS TO BECOMING A
## SUCCESSFUL STEWARD OF GOD —

**Step #1 — You must make a quality decision today to become faithful to your God in all things!**

Don't procrastinate. The Bible says people who are quick to respond to God's direction in giving are indispensable to Him.

> **. . . for God loves (He takes pleasure in, prizes above other things, and *is unwilling to abandon or to do without*) a cheerful (joyous, "prompt-to-do-it") giver. . . .**
>
> **2 Corinthians 9:7 Amplified**

Those who would be indispensable stewards of their God must never think the following thought. *"When I am able, I will tithe. When I have more seed, I will sow. When I accumulate a surplus, I will give."* The Bible says you cannot wait until you feel your circumstances are right to become faithful in your stewardship.

> **If you wait for perfect conditions, you will never get anything done.**
>
> **Ecclesiastes 11:4 TLB**

You must begin right now, no matter how little you may presently have, for Jesus says he that is faithful when there is little will also be faithful when he controls much (Luke 16:10).

You will never be able to make a quality, lasting decision to be faithful to God unless you realize that *God will be totally faithful to you.* As you move into the realm of being faithful with your giving to God, you will be exhibiting to the world how faithful God is to His children.

> **God is faithful (reliable, trustworthy, and therefore ever true to His promise, and He can be depended on); by Him you were called into companionship and participation with His Son, Jesus Christ our Lord.**
>
> **1 Corinthians 1:9 Amplified**

Children of the rich and faithful God of heaven openly display to the world that their God is trustworthy.

Confidence in God and His Word brings every steward of God to a place of complete trust in the leading of the Holy Spirit. This trust in the Holy Spirit's direction as it pertains to releasing finances brings all faithful stewards into an extremely intimate relationship with God. They become sons and daughters of God.

> **For as many as are led by the Spirit of God, they are the sons of God.**
>
> **Romans 8:14**

Being constantly led by the Holy Spirit also assures faithful stewards that each seed they sow moves them ever closer in this relationship.

### Step #2 — You must become faithful in small amounts.

Don't be discouraged if the little you have seems insignificant compared to the size of the Kingdom project before you. You must become convinced that even if your seed is small, it will be big in the eyes of God. It will do big things for you and your stewardship. So if the devil is trying to tell you the small amount you have in your hand isn't enough to really count with God, let him know that anyone can count the seeds in an apple, but no one can count all the apples in one little apple seed. Never allow yourself to become discouraged by any man or devil when you have only a little bit to sow, for when you plant even a small amount of seed in good ground, it brings forth a multiplied return. As a steward you must learn to be more focused on the size of the harvest that awaits you than you are on any temporary shortage you may be experiencing when God asks you to sow.

**He that goeth forth . . . bearing precious seed, shall doubtless come again with rejoicing, bringing his sheaves with him.**

**Psalm 126:6**

Sowing what you have, even if it is precious little, is overwhelming evidence to God that you trust Him. Think about it. You trusted God with your soul when you accepted Jesus as your Savior, so doesn't it make sense that you can also trust God when it comes to sowing into His Kingdom? Always remember God cannot lie.

**. . . [God] cannot lie.**

**Titus 1:2**

Because of this, you can know beyond any shadow of a doubt that He will honor His Word and return an increase to you for all you release to Him.

**Step #3 — You must prove yourself extra careful in money matters.**

You must learn to be extremely faithful in everyday money matters like paying your bills. You must diligently work at getting out of debt and staying out of debt. It is important that you prove yourself to be altogether trustworthy in money matters, knowing the money you are handling is not just any money; it's Kingdom money.

**. . . it is required in stewards, that a man be found faithful.**

**1 Corinthians 4:2**

Notice this verse does not speak of instantaneous approval of a person's stewardship, for there is always a season of proving before a proper biblical stewardship can be established. Do not become impatient, for your diligence will be rewarded with the fulfillment of God's promises.

**. . . be . . . followers of them who through faith and patience inherit the promises.**

**Hebrews 6:12**

Remember, in God's Kingdom, the only thing that happens instantly is the forgiveness of your sins through the blood of Jesus Christ. However, in the other matters of the Kingdom of God, we all have to grow up into that which God has planned for our individual lives. It is possible that you have developed some destructive habits in your life, habits you will have to overcome before God will be able to fully trust you as His steward. For instance, if you repeatedly spend more than your income allows, God will want you to bring that undisciplined behavior under control before He will trust you with significant amounts of His Kingdom money.

As you move forward in overcoming unscriptural methods of operation, God will increase the amount He entrusts to you. You must take proper care of the things God places into your control by keeping equipment properly maintained, clean, and neat. If you can't be faithful in maintaining an old automobile, why would God give you a new one to neglect and devaluate? Why would He give you several pairs of shoes if you neglect the one pair you have? This same concern for proper maintenance of clothing, houses, offices, business equipment, etc. is absolutely essential to anyone who wants true advancement to come to his stewardship.

Knowing that God is fair and just should allow you to depend on Him, being confident that He will give you time and assistance to become the person He envisions you to be. This process of renewal takes place as you take off the old man, the person you were before you were born again, and put on the new man that is formed in the likeness of God's own Son.

> **. . . put off concerning the former conversation the old man, which is corrupt according to the deceitful lusts;**
>
> **And be renewed in the spirit of your mind;**
>
> **And that ye put on the new man, which after God is created in righteousness and true holiness.**
>
> **Ephesians 4:22-24**

As you put on this new mindset, you will find it becomes progressively easier to please God.

### Step #4 — You must prove yourself faithful in that which belongs to others.

Before becoming a full-fledged steward of the rich God of heaven, God requires that you serve an apprenticeship as a faithful steward over that which belongs to someone other than yourself. Jesus says, "*. . . if ye have not been faithful in that which is another man's, who shall give you that which is your own?*" Luke 16:12

Part of the proof that God can trust you with the precious things of His Kingdom will come as He observes your faithfulness in handling someone else's possessions. They might be the possessions of your neighbors, friends, or fellow church members. For instance, if you share a ride to work, respect the automobile you are riding in. At church, show extra care and concern for the pews and other church property. If you borrow anything from a neighbor or friend, always return it in as good or better condition than when you received it. As you do this, God will see that you have the ability to care for things that belong to others. From this He will see how you will take care of that which belongs to Him.

Go back to the Garden of Eden, and you will see this identical plan in motion.

> **And the LORD God planted a garden eastward in Eden; and there he put the man whom he had formed.**
>
> **And out of the ground made the LORD God to grow every tree that is pleasant to the sight, and good for food; the tree of life also in the midst of the garden, and the tree of knowledge of good and evil.**
>
> **And the LORD God took the man, and put him into the garden of Eden to dress it and to keep it.**
>
> **Genesis 2:8-9,15**

It becomes obvious from this account that a big part of God's purpose for mankind was that of supervision and maintenance of that which belonged to His Kingdom. In the very beginning, we see that God gave Adam and Eve the responsibility of nurturing and caring for His garden. Notice God provided the garden to Adam and Eve for their enjoyment. However, there was a requirement involved. Adam would have to be a faithful steward over the garden. Understanding this divine principle is a vital part of being a co-laborer with God in His Kingdom.

God's plan for you to prosper and increase everything that He puts in your hand is always dependent on how careful you are in caring for that which belongs to someone else. It is no secret that God is seeking faithful sons and daughters to represent Him in this earth. He has chosen you by divine appointment to be His personal representative. The successful establishment of your stewardship is of great importance to Him as well as yourself. Because of this, you must remain directly in the center of God's plan for your life. Biblical stewardship involves much more than just making you rich. It consists of an ongoing relationship that God wants to establish with you. God's purpose for having you become a proper steward can be summed up in His desire for Father Abraham.

> . . . I will bless thee . . . and in thee shall all families of the earth be blessed.
>
> **Genesis 12:2,3**

With this ancient promise, God set forth the blueprint of His purpose for all of His faithful children. They would be given abundance to fulfill the desire of His heart, which is bringing lost mankind back into relationship with Him and back into the abundant life for which He originally created them. In all of this we can see the inner working of the heart of the truly rich God of heaven whose only desire for mankind is their salvation and their restoration into the good life God has planned for each of them.

It has nothing to do with the clouded theology of the poor god and his children's endless fundraising projects. The pure, unselfish desire of the rich God cries out from every page of the Bible as He speaks of His real purpose for humanity.

> **For God so loved the world, that he gave his only begotten Son, that whosoever believeth in him should not perish, but have everlasting life.**
>
> **John 3:16**

For the Son of man is come to seek and to save that which was lost.

**Luke 19:10**

. . . I am come that they might have life, and that they might have it more abundantly.

**John 10:10**

Only be thou strong and very courageous, that thou mayest observe to do according to all the law, which Moses my servant commanded thee: turn not from it to the right hand or to the left, that thou mayest prosper whithersoever thou goest.

This book of the law shall not depart out of thy mouth; but thou shalt meditate therein day and night, that thou mayest observe to do according to all that is written therein: for then thou shalt make thy way prosperous, and then thou shalt have good success.

**Joshua 1:7,8**

*As a child of the rich God of heaven,*
*you have a God-given right*
*to have all your needs and desires*
*supplied through your relationship*
*with His rich Son, Jesus Christ*

# KINGDOM KEYS TO THE GOOD LIFE

## CHAPTER 8

Now that you are well on your way to becoming a steward of the rich God of heaven, here are some very important keys to help keep you on the right path. Following these steps will help insure a continual flow of blessings into your stewardship.

### Key #1
### You Must Tithe

The tithe belongs to God.

> **And all the tithe of the land, whether of the seed of the land, or of the fruit of the tree, is the LORD'S: it is holy unto the LORD.**
>
> **Leviticus 27:30**

God promises that if you faithfully tithe, He will open heaven over your life and abundantly bless you.

> **Bring ye all the tithes into the storehouse, that there may be meat in mine house, and prove me now herewith, saith the LORD of hosts, if I will not open you the windows of heaven, and pour you out a blessing, that there shall not be room enough to receive it.**
>
> **Malachi 3:10**

## Key #2
### You Must Keep Your Priorities Right

You will not receive increase from God if you are asking for the wrong reasons.

> **Ye ask, and receive not, because you ask amiss, that ye may consume it upon your lusts.**
>
> **James 4:3**

You can be assured of an ever-increasing flow of wealth if you will always put the Kingdom of God first in your life.

> **But seek ye first the kingdom of God, and his righteousness; and all these things shall be added unto you.**
>
> **Matthew 6:33**

## Key #3
### You Must not Be Double Minded

A double-minded person cannot receive from God.

> **. . . he that wavereth is like a wave of the sea driven with the wind and tossed.**
>
> **For let not that man think that he shall receive any thing of the Lord.**
>
> **A double minded man is unstable in all his ways.**
>
> **James 1:6-8**

You can overcome double-mindedness by keeping all commitments, seriously studying God's Word, and exposing yourself to the Word of God as it is spoken by anointed ministers of God.

> **For I long to see you, that I may impart unto you some spiritual gift, *to the end ye may be established.***
>
> **Romans 1:11**

Constant input by the Word of God and His anointed preachers will result in your being solidly established in the things of God as well as the proper development of your stewardship.

### Key #4
### Your Offerings Must Be Acceptable to God

God only accepts offerings that are given from a willing heart in accordance with God's goodness to you.

**For if there be first a willing mind, it [your offering] is accepted according to that a man hath, and not according to that he hath not.**

**2 Corinthians 8:12**

Never give according to your circumstances. Always give in accordance with God's goodness and His instructions to you in giving.

### Key #5
### You Must Have Proper Understanding

Understanding always governs every part of your ability to receive from God.

**Beloved, I wish above all things that thou mayest prosper and be in health, even as thy soul [or understanding] prospereth.**

**3 John 2**

Don't blindly follow without understanding. If you don't understand something that's being taught, search it out afterwards. If you can't come up with a proper understanding of it from the study of your notes, get a tape of the lesson and study it again. If you still don't understand, don't be intimidated. Ask questions of those who watch over your soul, such as your pastor or an elder in your local church. However, always wait to ask your questions at the appropriate time.

**Ask, and it shall be given you; seek, and ye shall find; knock, and it shall be opened unto you:**

**For every one that asketh receiveth; and he that seeketh findeth; and to him that knocketh it shall be opened.**

**Matthew 7:7,8**

### Key #6
### You Must Cast Out All Fear

The spirit of fear does not come from God.

**For God hath not given us the spirit of fear; but of power, and of love, and of a sound mind.**

**2 Timothy 1:7**

Fear is overcome by trusting God's Word more than you trust anything else, Satan included.

**Casting down imaginations, and every high thing that exalteth itself against the knowledge of God, and bringing into captivity every thought to the obedience of Christ.**

**2 Corinthians 10:5**

Put up some no parking zones in your mind, not allowing the spirit of fear to hang around. Stay full of God's promises of your victory by constantly rehearsing who you really are in Christ Jesus.

You are more than a conqueror through Christ who strengthens you (Romans 8:37). You are mighty to the pulling down of strongholds (2 Corinthians 10:4). Nothing shall by any means harm you (Luke 10:19). If God is for you, who can stand against you (Romans 8:31)? These and other truths about you from God's Word will dispel the darkness of fear and release the powerful light of faith upon the pathway of your life.

## Key #7
## You Must Have Faith

Faith pleases God.

> **But without faith it is impossible to please him: for he that cometh to God must believe that he is, and that he is a rewarder of them that diligently seek him.**
>
> **Hebrews 11:6**

Strong faith is absolutely necessary for divine increase because your unwavering faith is the raw material from which every promise of God is made.

> **Now faith is the substance [raw material] of things hoped for, the evidence of things not seen.**
>
> **Hebrews 11:1**

Jesus tells us the funding of your stewardship will take place in direct proportion to the strength of your faith.

> **. . . According to your faith and trust and reliance [on the power invested in Me] be it done to you.**
>
> **Matthew 9:29 Amplified**

## Key #8
## You Must Cast Down All Unbelief

Unbelief will keep you from receiving God's promised blessings.

> **So we see that they were not able to enter [into His rest],
> because of their unwillingness to adhere to and trust in and rely
> on God [unbelief had shut them out].**
>
> **Hebrews 3:19 Amplified**

Unbelief comes quickly to those who do not keep a record of past victories in the forefront of their minds. Jesus said there is great power for overcoming the devil and his tricks when you rehearse past victories.

> **. . . they overcame him by the blood of the Lamb and by the
> word of their testimony. . . .**
>
> **Revelation 12:11**

## Key #9
## You Must not Look Back to Your Old Life

You must release the things of the past. Whether they were good or bad, they are over. However, your whole eternity is ahead of you, and in Christ your future looks very bright. Jesus wants the things that you are about to do for Him to be the most important things in your life. There are no "good old days" in your pre-Christ existence. There are only untold multitudes of "good new days" ahead.

> **Jesus said to him, No one who puts his hand to the plow and
> looks back [to the things behind] is fit for the kingdom of God.**
>
> **Luke 9:62 Amplified**

Also keep in mind that our Lord always saves the best wine for last. It is exactly as the old gospel hymn stated, "Sweeter gets the journey every day. Serving Jesus really pays."

## Key #10
## If Married, You Must Maintain a
## Proper Marriage Relationship

A turbulent marriage will cause your prayers to be hindered. Hindered prayers stop your communication with God, causing His abundance into your stewardship to be interrupted.

**Likewise, ye husbands, dwell with them according to knowledge, giving honor unto the wife, as unto the weaker vessel, and as being heirs together of the grace of life; that your prayers be not hindered.**

**1 Peter 3:7**

## Key #11
## You Must Keep a Proper Relationship
## with Your Spiritual Leaders

No matter how tempting it might become not to submit to a proper pastor, it is a major mistake and stumbling block to the steward of God. It is of the greatest importance that you have a good report from those who oversee you in Christ.

**Obey your spiritual leaders and submit to them [continually recognizing their authority over you], for they are constantly keeping watch over your souls and guarding your spiritual welfare, as men who will have to render an account [of their trust]. [Do your part to] let them do this with gladness and not with sighing and groaning, for that would not be profitable to you [either].**

**Hebrews 13:17 Amplified**

## Key #12
### You Must Walk in Love

Do not allow strife or bitterness into your relationship with your Christian brothers and sisters. These unchristian attitudes will stop the increase that you are expecting from your sowing.

**Therefore if thou bring thy gift to the altar, and there rememberest that thy brother hath ought against thee;**

**Leave there thy gift before the altar, and go thy way; first be reconciled to thy brother, and then come and offer thy gift.**

**Matthew 5:23,24**

The Christ life as well as the Christ-like attitude toward all your brothers and sisters in the Lord is a big part of operating a proper stewardship for God.

## Key #13
### You Must Believe the Proven Ministers of God

The Bible tells us that believing God brings an establishment to your life. The Bible also tells us that believing God's proven ministers releases prosperity into your stewardship.

**. . . Hear me, O Judah, and ye inhabitants of Jerusalem; Believe in the LORD your God, so shall ye be established; believe his prophets, so shall ye prosper.**

**2 Chronicles 20:20**

If you are not in a good church, get into a good gospel preaching church as soon as possible. You should also get involved in a progressive ministry that focuses on faith and God's desire to prosper His children. Don't allow yourself to listen to everything religious that comes to you by radio, television, or in the form of tapes and books. Be as selective with your spiritual input as you would be with the input you would allow to come to your own children.

## Key #14
### You Must Be Willing to Work Hard

God says that you will not be allowed to prosper in His economy if you won't work.

> **For even when we were with you, this we commanded you, that if any would not work, neither should he eat.**
>
> **2 Thessalonians 3:10**

You must also understand that the Bible says the number one reason for working is that you may have money for sowing.

> **Let him that stole steal no more: but rather let him labor, working with his hands the thing which is good, that he may have to give to him that needeth.**
>
> **Ephesians 4:28**

Never underestimate this truth, for without seed (money) for giving (sowing), you would not be able to have a financial harvest.

## Key #15
### You Must Keep Sin Out of Your Life

You must be careful not to allow sin to take up its dwelling with you, for right standing with God is a prerequisite to receiving God's blessings.

And it shall come to pass, if thou shalt hearken diligently unto the voice of the LORD thy God, to observe and to do all his commandments which I command thee this day, that the LORD thy God will set thee on high above all nations of the earth:

And all these blessings shall come on thee, and overtake thee, if thou shalt hearken unto the voice of the LORD thy God.

**Deuteronomy 28:1,2**

## Key #16
## You Must Speak Properly

As a proper steward, you must guard your words, speaking only of health, life, prosperity, and the godly desires that your Heavenly Father places in your heart. Remember the Lord Jesus Himself told us we would have what we say.

For verily I say unto you, That whosoever shall say unto this mountain, Be thou removed, and be thou cast into the sea; and shall not doubt in his heart, but shall believe that those things which he saith shall come to pass; he shall have whatsoever he saith.

**Mark 11:23**

## Key #17
## You Must Faithfully Pay Your Pledges to God

Unpaid vows to ministers or ministries cause God to categorize a person as a fool.

When thou vowest a vow unto God, defer not to pay it; for he hath no pleasure in fools: pay that which thou hast vowed.

**Eccesiastes 5:4**

God will not prosper the foolish, for the Bible says they will, by their own foolishness, keep themselves from prospering.

**There is treasure to be desired and oil in the dwelling of the wise; but a foolish man spendeth it up.**

**Proverbs 21:20**

### Key #18
### You Must Keep a Right Perception of God

Make it a point to always perceive God to be who the Bible says He is. Our God is the rich generous God of heaven. He is the one who desires to bless, not curse His children. Use scriptures such as the 23rd Psalm as a guide to His goodness and abundant supply.

**The Lord is my shepherd; I shall not want.**

**He maketh me to lie down in green pastures: he leadeth me beside the still waters.**

**He restoreth my soul: he leadeth me in the paths of righteousness for his name's sake.**

**Yea, though I walk through the valley of the shadow of death, I will fear no evil: for thou art with me; thy rod and thy staff they comfort me.**

**Thou preparest a table before me in the presence of mine enemies: thou anointest my head with oil; my cup runneth over.**

**Surely goodness and mercy shall follow me all the days of my life: and I will dwell in the house of the Lord for ever.**

**Psalm 23**

## Key #19
### You Must not Love Money

The love of money is the root of all evil. This simply means that loving money is the first step toward most sins.

**For the love of money is the root of all evil: which while some coveted after, they have erred from the faith, and pierced themselves through with many sorrows.**

**1 Timothy 6:10**

Money is not for loving. It is for blessing you and your family as well as all the families of the earth (Genesis 12:1-3).

## Key #20
### You Must Respond to the Cry of the Poor

You must become fully aware of the fact that giving to the poor is actually an interaction between you and your Lord, for when you give to the poor, you are lending to God.

**He that hath pity upon the poor lendeth unto the LORD; and that which he hath given will he pay him again.**

**Proverbs 19:17**

Turning a deaf ear to the poor will bring you to a time of need, and worst of all, no one will respond to your cry for help.

**Whoso stoppeth his ears at the cry of the poor, he also shall cry himself, but shall not be heard.**

**Proverbs 21:13**

### Key #21
### You Must Be a Faithful Doer of the Word

It is the doer of God's Word that receives God's blessing.

**But be ye doers of the word, and not hearers only, deceiving your own selves.**

**But whoso looketh into the perfect law of liberty, and continueth therein, he being not a forgetful hearer, but a doer of the work,** *this man shall be blessed in his deed.*

**James 1:22,25**

### Key #22
### You Must Rid Yourself of
### Traditional Thinking About Money

Traditional thinking about money will render God's truth about it ineffective.

**So for the sake of your tradition (the rules handed down by your forefathers), you have set aside the Word of God [depriving it of force and authority and making it of no effect].**

**Matthew 15:6 Amplified**

Whenever the Word of God becomes of no effect through a tradition, none of its benefits can flow to the child of God. Keep all traditional thinking out of your mind, and allow God's best into your life.

### Key #23
### You Must Learn to Exercise Patience

The full transformation of your perception of God from a poor god to a rich God will probably take a period of time. Just be patient, for sowing seed may not bring an instant harvest. It takes time for the seed to grow to maturity.

> . . . So is the kingdom of God, as if a man should cast seed into the ground;

> And should sleep, and rise night and day, and the seed should spring and grow up, he knoweth not how.

> For the earth bringeth forth fruit of herself; first the blade, then the ear, after that the full corn in the ear.

> **Mark 4:26-28**

As you exercise patience, be assured by God's Word you will receive the harvest God promises.

> . . . ye have need of patience, that, after ye have done the will of God, ye might receive the promise.

> **Hebrews 10:36**

## Key #24
### Remember the Best Harvest Is Always Saved for Last

As I pen this final key, I go far beyond any earthly harvest into the final harvest of every good and faithful steward. I go all the way to the great harvest of God's judgment.

> When the Son of man shall come in his glory, and all the holy angels with him, then shall he sit upon the throne of his glory:

> And before him shall be gathered all nations: and he shall separate them one from another, as a shepherd divideth his sheep from the goats:

And he shall set the sheep on his right hand, but the goats on the left.

Then shall the King say unto them on his right hand, Come, ye blessed of my Father, inherit the kingdom prepared for you from the foundation of the world:

For I was an hungered, and ye gave me meat: I was thirsty, and ye gave me drink: I was a stranger, and ye took me in:

Naked, and ye clothed me: I was sick, and ye visited me: I was in prison, and ye came unto me.

Then shall the righteous answer him, saying, Lord, when saw we thee an hungered, and fed thee? Or thirsty, and gave thee drink?

When saw we thee a stranger, and took thee in? or naked, and clothed thee?

Or when saw we thee sick, or in prison, and came unto thee?

And the King shall answer and say unto them, Verily I say unto you, Inasmuch as ye have done it unto one of the least of these my brethren, ye have done it unto me.

Matthew 25:31-40

— TAKING ACTION —

It is now time for you to act upon the truth you have learned from the Word of God.

The God of heaven is rich not poor. You, as a child of the rich God of heaven, have a God-given right to have all of your needs as well as your desires supplied through your blood-bought relationship with His rich Son, Jesus Christ. You are standing at the threshold of a bright new future as a steward in the rich Kingdom of your rich God.

You must never forget that you will have the God you perceive. You will live with the consequences that come with a poor god if you perceive that your god is after your money. You will live with the benefits of a rich God if you believe that He is trying to get money to you. Your perceptions of God and His desire for your finances will cause Him to be either Jehovah Needy or Jehovah Jireh.

According to the Bible, God is Jehovah-Jireh, the God who abundantly provides for His children. He is not Jehovah Needy, the god whose children must provide for him. According to the Word of God, He is the God that is ready, willing and able to prosper and abundantly bless you beyond your ability to even imagine.

Here is what this book is all about in a nutshell. You are a living epistle that is being read by all of the lost people that observe your life.

**. . . you yourselves are our letter of recommendation (our credentials), written in your hearts, to be known (perceived, recognized) and read by everybody.**

**2 Corinthians 3:2 Amplified**

If you perceive from the teaching of the leaders of organized religion that God is in need of your money, all who observe you will perceive your god to be needy or greedy, causing them to draw away from him. However, if the God you perceive from a correct understanding of His Word is one who abundantly blesses and prospers His children, those who observe His goodness to you and through you will perceive Him to be a good God, a gracious Creator who willingly supplies and blesses His children. This, like nothing else, will draw people to your God so that they can also be blessed.

In closing, please join the Apostle Paul in making the following affirmation. Let it be the beginning of a wonderful new vocation as God's steward.

I pray that the rich God of heaven would grant you, according to the riches of his glory, to be strengthened with might by his Spirit in the inner man;

That Christ may dwell in your hearts by faith; that ye, being rooted and grounded in love,

May be able to comprehend with all saints what is the breadth, and length, and depth, and height;

And to know the love of Christ, which passeth knowledge, that ye might be filled with all the fulness of God.

Now unto him that is able to do exceeding abundantly above all that we ask or think, according to the power that worketh in us,

Unto him be glory in the church by Christ Jesus throughout all ages, world without end. Amen.

Adapted from Ephesians 3:16-21

***God Jehovah is in fact the Rich God of Heaven!***

BOOKS BY JOHN AVANZINI

*30, 60, Hundredfold*

*Always Abounding*

*Basics of Abundance*

*Breakthrough for Unanswered Prayer*

*Debt Terminator Kit*

*Faith Extenders*

*Financial Excellence*

*God's Debt Free Guarantee*

*It's Not Working Brother John*

*John Avanzini Answers Your Questions*

*Powerful Principles of Increase*

*Stolen Property Returned*

*Things that are Better than Money*

*Wealth of the World*

*What Jesus Taught about Manifesting Abundance*

*War on Debt*

*Rapid Debt Reduction Strategies*

*The Victory Book*

*Have a Good Report*

*A Word Fitly Spoken Series*

*The Principles of Increase Series*

**Available at your local bookstore.**
**Abel Press - Tulsa, Oklahoma**

To contact this ministry, write to:

John Avanzini Ministries

P.O. Box 917001

Fort Worth, TX 76117-9001

www.avanzini.org